Active Machine Learning with Python

Refine and elevate data quality over quantity with active learning

Margaux Masson-Forsythe

Active Machine Learning with Python

Copyright © 2024 Packt Publishing

Group Product Manager: Niranjan Naikwadi

Publishing Product Manager: Tejashwini R

Book Project Manager: Kirti Pisat

Senior Editor: Vandita Grover

Technical Editor: Rahul Limbachiya

Copy Editor: Safis Editing

Proofreader: Safis Editing

Indexer: Manju Arasan

Production Designer: Vijay Kamble

DevRel Marketing Coordinator: Vinishka Kalra

First published: March 2024
Production reference: 1270324

Published by Packt Publishing Ltd.
Grosvenor House
11 St Paul's Square
Birmingham
B3 1RB, UK.

ISBN 978-1-83546-494-6

www.packtpub.com

About the reviewer

Mourya Boggarapa is a deep learning software engineer specializing in the end-to-end integration of large language models for custom AI accelerators. He holds a master's degree in software engineering from Carnegie Mellon University. Prior to his current role, Mourya honed his skills through diverse experiences: developing backend systems for a major bank, building development infrastructure for a tech giant, and some mobile app development. He cultivated a comprehensive understanding of software development across various domains. His primary passion lies in deep learning. Additionally, he maintains a keen interest in human-computer interaction, aiming to bridge the gap between tech and human experience.

Table of Contents

Preface   xi

Part 1: Fundamentals of Active Machine Learning

1

Introducing Active Machine Learning   3

Understanding active machine
learning systems   3

Definition   4

Potential range of applications   4

Key components of active machine
learning systems   5

Exploring query strategies scenarios   7

Membership query synthesis   7

Stream-based selective sampling   8

Pool-based sampling   11

Comparing active and
passive learning   13

Summary   14

2

Designing Query Strategy Frameworks   17

Technical requirements   18

Exploring uncertainty
sampling methods   18

Understanding query-by-
committee approaches   25

Maximum disagreement   26

Vote entropy   28

Average KL divergence   30

Labeling with EMC sampling   34

Sampling with EER   37

Understanding density-
weighted sampling methods   38

Summary   44

3

Managing the Human in the Loop   45

Technical requirements	45	Effectively managing human-in-the-loop systems	55
Designing interactive learning systems and workflows	46		
Exploring human-in-the-loop labeling tools	50	Ensuring annotation quality and dataset balance	57
Common labeling platforms	51	Assess annotator skills	57
		Use multiple annotators	58
Handling model-label disagreements	52	Balanced sampling	59
Programmatically identifying mismatches	52	Summary	61
Manual review of conflicts	54		

Part 2: Active Machine Learning in Practice

4

Applying Active Learning to Computer Vision   65

Technical requirements	65	Preparing and training our model	77
Implementing active ML for an image classification project	66	Analyzing the evaluation metrics	79
		Implementing an active ML strategy	80
Building a CNN for the CIFAR dataset	67	Using active ML for a segmentation project	84
Applying uncertainty sampling to improve classification performance	73	Summary	88
Applying active ML to an object detection project	76		

5

Leveraging Active Learning for Big Data   89

Technical requirements	89	Selecting the most informative frames with Lightly	92
Implementing ML models for video analysis	90		

Using Lightly to select the best frames
to label for object detection   93

SSL with active ML   115

Summary   **118**

Part 3: Applying Active Machine Learning to Real-World Projects

6

Evaluating and Enhancing Efficiency   121

Technical requirements   **121**

**Creating efficient active
ML pipelines**   **122**

Monitoring active ML pipelines   **124**

**Determining when to stop
active ML runs**   **127**

**Enhancing production model
monitoring with active ML**   **128**

Challenges in monitoring
production models   128

Active ML to monitor models
in production   130

Early detection for data drift and
model decay   132

Summary   **133**

7

Utilizing Tools and Packages for Active ML   135

Technical requirements   **135**

**Mastering Python packages
for enhanced active ML**   **136**

scikit-learn   136

modAL   139

**Getting familiar with
the active ML tools**   **145**

Summary   **147**

Index   149

Other Books You May Enjoy   156

Preface

Welcome to *Active Learning with Python* a comprehensive guide designed to introduce you to the power of active machine learning. This book is written with the conviction that while data is plentiful, its quality and relevance hold the key to building models that are not only efficient but also robust and insightful.

Active machine learning is a method used in machine learning where the algorithm can query an oracle to label new data points with the desired outputs. It stands at the crossroads of optimization and human-computer interaction, enabling machines to learn more effectively with less data. This is particularly valuable in scenarios where data labeling is costly, time-consuming, or requires expert knowledge.

Throughout this book, we leverage Python, a leading programming language in the field of data science and machine learning, known for its simplicity and powerful libraries. Python serves as an excellent medium for exploring the concepts of active machine learning, providing both beginners and experienced practitioners with the tools needed to implement sophisticated models.

Who this book is for

This book is intended for data scientists, machine learning engineers, researchers, and anyone curious about optimizing machine learning workflows. Whether you are new to active machine learning or looking to enhance your current models, this book provides insights into making the most of your data through strategic querying and learning techniques.

What this book covers

Chapter 1, Introducing Active Machine Learning, explores the fundamental principles of active machine learning, a highly effective approach that significantly differs from passive methods. This chapter also offers insights into its distinctive strategies and advantages.

Chapter 2, Designing Query Strategy Frameworks, presents a comprehensive exploration of the most effective and widely utilized query strategy frameworks in active machine learning and covers uncertainty sampling, query-by-committee, expected model change, expected error reduction, and density-weighted methods.

Chapter 3, Managing the Human in the Loop, discusses the best practices and techniques for the design of interactive active machine learning systems, with an emphasis on optimizing human-in-the-loop labeling. Aspects such as labeling interface design, the crafting of effective workflows, strategies for resolving model-label disagreements, the selection of suitable labelers, and their efficient management are covered.

Chapter 4, Applying Active Learning to Computer Vision, covers various techniques for harnessing the power of active machine learning to enhance computer vision model performance in tasks such as image classification, object detection, and semantic segmentation, also addressing the challenges in their application.

Chapter 5, Leveraging Active Learning for Big Data, explores the active machine learning techniques for managing big data such as videos, and acknowledges the challenges in developing video analysis models due to their large size and frequent data duplication based on frames-per-second rates, with a demonstration of an active machine learning method for selecting the most informative frames for labeling.

Chapter 6, Evaluating and Enhancing Efficiency, details the evaluation of active machine learning systems, encompassing metrics, automation, efficient labeling, testing, monitoring, and stopping criteria, aiming for accurate evaluations and insights into system efficiency, guiding informed improvements in the field.

Chapter 7, Utilizing Tools and Packages for Active ML, discusses the Python libraries, frameworks, and tools commonly used for active learning, highlighting their value in implementing various active learning techniques and offering an overview suitable for both beginners and experienced programmers.

To get the most out of this book

You should possess proficiency in Python coding and familiarity with Google Colab, alongside a foundational understanding of machine learning and deep learning principles. You also need to be familiar with machine learning frameworks like PyTorch.

This book is for individuals who possess a fundamental understanding of machine learning and deep learning and who aim to acquire knowledge about active learning in order to optimize the annotation process of their machine learning datasets. This optimization will enable them to train the most effective models possible.

Software covered in the book
Python packages: `scikit-learn`, `matplotlib`, `numpy`, `datasets`, `transformers`, `huggingface_hub`, `torch`, `pandas`, `torchvision`, `roboflow`, `tqdm`, `glob`, `pyyaml`, `opencv-python`, `ultralytics`, `lightly`, `docker`, `encord`, `clearml`, `pymongo`, and `modAL-python`
Jupyter or Google Colab notebook (with Python version 3.10.12 and above)

You will need to create accounts for diverse tools: **Encord**, **Roboflow**, and **Lightly**. You will also need access to an **AWS EC2 instance** for *Chapter 6, Evaluating and Enhancing Efficiency*.

If you are using the digital version of this book, we advise you to type the code yourself or access the code from the book's GitHub repository (a link is available in the next section). Doing so will help you avoid any potential errors related to the copying and pasting of code.

Download the example code files

You can download the example code files for this book from GitHub at `https://github.com/PacktPublishing/Active-Machine-Learning-with-Python`. If there's an update to the code, it will be updated in the GitHub repository.

We also have other code bundles from our rich catalog of books and videos available at `https://github.com/PacktPublishing/`. Check them out!

Conventions used

There are a number of text conventions used throughout this book.

`Code in text`: Indicates code words in text, database table names, folder names, filenames, file extensions, pathnames, dummy URLs, user input, and Twitter handles. Here is an example: "We define `x_true` and `y_true`."

A block of code is set as follows:

```
y_true = np.array(small_dataset['label'])
x_true = np.array(small_dataset['text'])
```

Bold: Indicates a new term, an important word, or words that you see onscreen. For instance, words in menus or dialog boxes appear in **bold**. Here is an example: "**Anomaly detection** is another domain where active learning proves to be highly effective."

> **Tips or important notes**
> Appear like this.

Get in touch

Feedback from our readers is always welcome.

General feedback: If you have questions about any aspect of this book, email us at customercare@packtpub.com and mention the book title in the subject of your message.

Errata: Although we have taken every care to ensure the accuracy of our content, mistakes do happen. If you have found a mistake in this book, we would be grateful if you would report this to us. Please visit www.packtpub.com/support/errata and fill in the form.

Piracy: If you come across any illegal copies of our works in any form on the internet, we would be grateful if you would provide us with the location address or website name. Please contact us at copyright@packt.com with a link to the material.

If you are interested in becoming an author: If there is a topic that you have expertise in and you are interested in either writing or contributing to a book, please visit authors.packtpub.com.

Share Your Thoughts

Once you've read *Active Machine Learning with Python*, we'd love to hear your thoughts! Scan the QR code below to go straight to the Amazon review page for this book and share your feedback.

https://packt.link/r/1835464947

Your review is important to us and the tech community and will help us make sure we're delivering excellent quality content.

Download a free PDF copy of this book

Thanks for purchasing this book!

Do you like to read on the go but are unable to carry your print books everywhere?

Is your eBook purchase not compatible with the device of your choice?

Don't worry, now with every Packt book you get a DRM-free PDF version of that book at no cost.

Read anywhere, any place, on any device. Search, copy, and paste code from your favorite technical books directly into your application.

The perks don't stop there, you can get exclusive access to discounts, newsletters, and great free content in your inbox daily

Follow these simple steps to get the benefits:

1. Scan the QR code or visit the link below

https://packt.link/free-ebook/9781835464946

2. Submit your proof of purchase
3. That's it! We'll send your free PDF and other benefits to your email directly

Part 1: Fundamentals of Active Machine Learning

In the rapidly evolving landscape of **machine learning** (ML), the concept of active ML has emerged as a transformative approach that optimizes the learning process by selectively querying the most informative data points from unlabeled datasets. This part of the book is dedicated to laying the foundational principles, strategies such as uncertainty sampling, query-by-committee, expected model change, expected error reduction, and density-weighted methods, and considerations essential for understanding and implementing active ML effectively. Through a structured exploration, we aim to equip readers with a solid grounding of the best practices for managing the human in the loop by exploring labeling interface design, effective workflows, strategies for handling model-label disagreements, finding adequate labelers, and managing them efficiently.

This part includes the following chapters:

- *Chapter 1, Introducing Active Machine Learning*
- *Chapter 2, Designing Query Strategy Frameworks*
- *Chapter 3, Managing the Human in the Loop*

1

Introducing Active Machine Learning

Machine learning models require large, labeled datasets, which can be expensive and time-consuming to obtain. **Active machine learning (active ML)** minimizes the labeling effort needed by intelligently choosing which data points a human should label. In this book, you will gain the necessary knowledge to understand active learning, including its mechanisms and applications. With these fundamentals, the subsequent chapters will equip you with concrete skills to implement active learning techniques on your own.

By the end of this book, you will have practical experience with state-of-the-art strategies to minimize labeling costs and maximize model performance. You will be able to apply active learning to enhance the efficiency and adaptability of your models across different application areas, such as vision and language.

To begin with, this chapter provides an introduction to active ML and explains how it can improve model accuracy using fewer labeled examples. By the end of the chapter, you will have covered the following:

- Understanding active machine learning systems
- Exploring query strategy scenarios
- Comparing active and passive learning

Understanding active machine learning systems

Active machine learning (active ML) is a powerful approach that seeks to create predictive models with remarkable accuracy, all while minimizing the number of labeled training examples required. This is achieved by employing a clever strategy that involves selectively choosing the most informative data points to be labeled by a knowledgeable oracle, such as a human annotator. By doing so, active learning enables models to extract the necessary knowledge they need from a relatively small amount of data.

Now, let's explore some definitions and the fundamental concepts that form the foundation of active ML.

Definition

Active learning can be defined as a dynamic and iterative approach to machine learning, where the algorithm intelligently engages with an **oracle** to label new data points. An oracle is a source that provides labels for data points queried by the active learner. The oracle acts as a teacher, guiding the model by providing labels for its most informative queries. Typically, oracles are human annotators or experts who can manually assign labels to new data points. However, oracles can also be simulation engines, crowdsourcing services, or other systems capable of labeling.

The key objective of active ML is to select and prioritize the most informative data points for the model. The aim is to achieve higher accuracy levels while minimizing the need for extensive training labels, in comparison to traditional supervised learning methods, which rely on large datasets of pre-labeled examples to train models in predicting outcomes. On the other hand, unsupervised learning methods work with unlabeled data, seeking patterns or structures without explicit instruction on the outcomes. Active learning bridges these approaches by focusing on a semi-supervised learning strategy. This process allows the model to actively learn and adapt over time, continuously improving its predictive capabilities by leveraging the most relevant and significant data points. By actively engaging with the data and carefully choosing which samples to label, active ML optimizes the entire learning process. It allows the algorithm to focus on the most relevant and informative instances, thereby reducing the need for extensive labeling efforts. As a result, active ML not only saves time and resources but also enables machine learning models to achieve higher accuracy and better generalization. Active ML opens the door for more advanced and intelligent machine learning systems by effectively prioritizing data labeling.

Potential range of applications

Active learning is a highly versatile technique that can significantly enhance efficiency and model performance across a wide range of applications. It does so by directing human labeling efforts to areas where they can have the most impact.

This approach has proven to be particularly effective in **computer vision applications**, such as image classification, object detection, and image segmentation. By selectively acquiring labels for ambiguous images that traditional sampling methods often miss, active learning can reduce costs and improve accuracy. It does this by identifying the most informative edge cases to query, allowing for accurate results with fewer labeled samples. For example, if we consider a self-driving car object-detection model that needs to identify various objects such as people, trees, and other cars, we can utilize active learning to prioritize the classes that it may struggle to learn.

In **natural language tasks**, such as document classification and translation, active learners play a crucial role in filling gaps in linguistic coverage. By querying sentences that cover rare vocabulary and structures, active learning improves adaptation and improves overall performance. The labeling process is focused only on the most useful examples, minimizing the need for extensive labeling efforts.

Anomaly detection is another domain where active learning proves to be highly effective. By targeting rare outliers and anomalies, which are critical for identifying issues such as fraud, active learning improves the detection of these important but uncommon examples. By focusing human reviews on unusual cases, active learning enhances the overall accuracy of anomaly detection systems.

Recommendation systems heavily rely on user feedback, and active learning provides a framework for acquiring this feedback intelligently. By querying users on their preferences for certain content, active learning gathers focused signals that can be used to fine-tune recommendations. For example, streaming services can use active learning techniques to improve the accuracy and relevance of their video suggestions.

In the field of **medical diagnosis**, active learning techniques play a vital role in minimizing physician time spent on common diagnoses. By identifying challenging cases that require expert input, active learning ensures that effort is focused on ambiguous examples that can significantly improve diagnostic model performance.

Active learning provides both the algorithms and mechanisms necessary to efficiently focus human effort on useful areas across various applications. By selectively acquiring labels, it overcomes the inherent costs and challenges associated with supervised machine learning, making it an invaluable tool in the field of artificial intelligence. Across science, engineering, and technology, the ability to intelligently guide data collection and labeling can accelerate progress with minimal human effort.

Now, let's move ahead to discuss the key components of an active learning system and how they apply to all the applications we have just mentioned.

Key components of active machine learning systems

Active ML systems comprise four key elements:

- **Unlabeled dataset**: This pool of unlabeled data points is what the active learner can query from. It may contain tens, hundreds, or even millions of examples.

- **Query strategy**: This is the core mechanism of active learning. It guides how the system selects which data points to query labels for. Different criteria can be used, which we will explore later.

- **Machine learning model**: The underlying predictive model being trained, such as a neural network, random forest, or SVM.

- **Oracle**: The source that provides labels. This is typically a human annotator who can manually label queried data points.

How do the key components just mentioned interact with each other? *Figure 1.1* depicts the interaction between various components of an active ML loop:

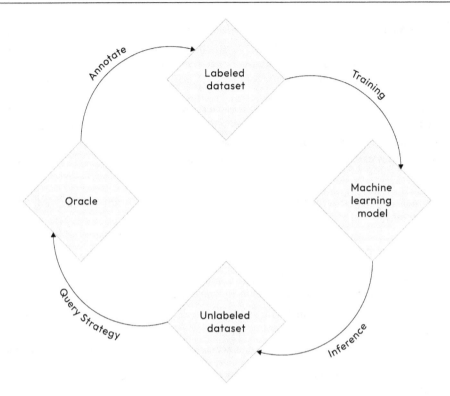

Figure 1.1 – Active ML loop

Models engage in an iterative loop, such as the following:

1. The query strategy identifies the most useful data points to label.

2. These are labeled by the oracle (human annotator).

3. The newly labeled data is used to train the machine learning model.

4. The updated model is then used to inform the next round of querying and labeling.

This loop allows active learning models to intelligently explore datasets, acquiring new training labels that maximize information gain.

In the next section, we will dig deeper into the query strategy step by first examining the various scenarios that one can choose from.

Exploring query strategies scenarios

Active learning can be implemented in different ways, depending on the nature of the unlabeled data and how the queries are performed. There are three main scenarios to consider when implementing active learning:

- Membership query synthesis
- Stream-based selective sampling
- Pool-based sampling

These scenarios offer different ways to optimize and improve the active learning process. Understanding these scenarios can help you make informed decisions and choose the most suitable approach for your specific needs. In this section, we will explore each of these scenarios.

Membership query synthesis

In **membership query synthesis**, the active learner has the ability to create its own unlabeled data points in order to improve its training. This is done by generating new data points from scratch and then requesting the oracle for labels, as depicted in *Figure 1.2*. By incorporating these newly labeled data points into its training set, the model becomes more robust and accurate:

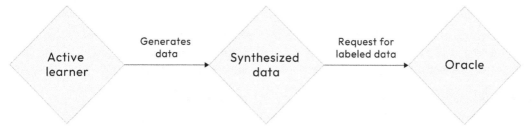

Figure 1.2 – Membership query synthesis workflow

Let's consider an image classifier as an example. With the power of synthesis, the active learner can create new images by combining various shapes, textures, and colors in different compositions. This allows the model to explore a wide range of possibilities and learn to recognize patterns and features that may not have been present in the original labeled data.

Similarly, a text classifier can also benefit from membership query synthesis. By generating new sentences and paragraphs with specific words or structures, the model can expand its understanding of different language patterns and improve its ability to classify text accurately.

There are several advantages of membership query synthesis:

- The model has complete control over the data points it queries, allowing it to focus on corner cases and unusual examples that normal sampling might overlook. This helps to reduce overfitting and improve the model's generalization by increasing the diversity of the data.

- By synthesizing data, the model can actively explore its weaknesses rather than rely on what is in the training data

- This is useful for problems where data synthesis is straightforward, such as simple tabular data and sequences.

However, there are also several disadvantages to using this scenario:

- It requires the ability to synthesize new useful data points accurately. This can be extremely difficult for complex real-world data such as images, audio, and video.

- Data synthesis does not work well for high-dimensional, nuanced data. The generated points are often not natural.

- It is less practical for real-world applications today compared to pool-based sampling. Advances in generative modeling can improve synthesis.

- It is computationally expensive to repeatedly generate full data points from scratch, especially for multimedia data.

- Over-generating synthetic examples can lead to overfitting, wherein the model becomes overly fixated on classifying the synthetic instances rather than the actual data. As a result, the model's accuracy may suffer when confronted with unfamiliar and unseen data.

Overall, membership query synthesis is mostly studied in theory and rarely applied in practice today. However, advances in generative modeling may increase its viability for real applications in the future.

Stream-based selective sampling

In **stream-based selective sampling**, the process of receiving unlabeled data points occurs continuously and dynamically rather than in a static and predetermined batch. *Figure 1.3* shows how the active learner is presented with a constant flow of data points, one after another:

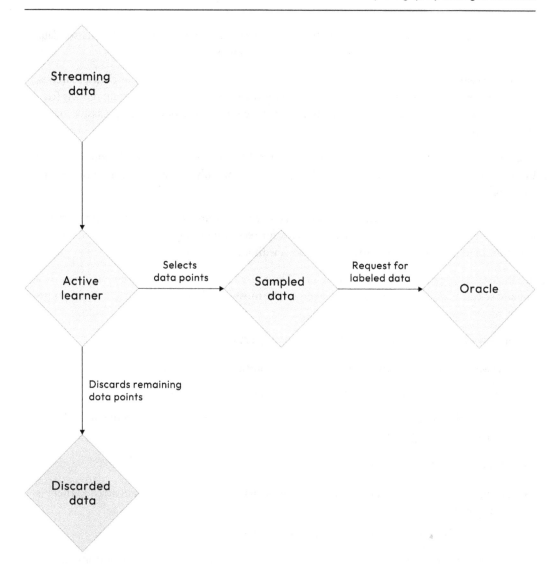

Figure 1.3 – Stream-based selective sampling workflow

The active learner is faced with the task of making instantaneous decisions about whether or not to request a label for each individual point. This real-time decision-making process adds an element of flexibility and adaptability to the learning algorithm. This allows it to adjust its sampling strategy on the fly based on the evolving characteristics of the incoming data stream. By actively selecting which data points to query for labels, the active learner can optimize the learning process and make the most efficient use of limited labeling resources.

Stream-based selective sampling finds its applications in data, including user activity, live sensor data, and the data in news feeds, social media, and many more sources.

There is a massive amount of data being generated by user activity in the form of clicks, searches, and posts. By selectively labeling a fraction of user actions on websites and apps to train models (e.g., predicting churn and engagement), stream-based selective sampling avoids storing massive logs of all user actions.

On the other hand, live sensor data from devices or machinery requires continual monitoring. To minimize this oversight, the querying of labels is performed on only the most critical sensor events from autonomous systems.

In the case of news feeds, social media streams, and content recommendation systems, stream-based selective sampling helps in acquiring user feedback for recommending a small fraction of content items. This focused user input improves suggestions without overwhelming the users.

In these cases, data arrives constantly in real time. The active learning model evaluates each new data point and selectively queries the oracle for labels on the most useful examples. The less useful points are discarded rather than stored.

The main advantages of stream-based selective sampling are the following:

- It is well-suited for real-time applications with constant live data streams
- It is storage efficient as the full data stream isn't saved, only the queried points
- It is scalable because it involves efficiently managing high volumes of incoming data without the need for storing all of it

However, it comes with a few drawbacks, too, listed as follows:

- The model must evaluate and make query decisions on the fly as the stream arrives. There is no opportunity for deep analysis.
- Discarded points cannot be revisited or re-queried later.
- Changes in data distribution over time are harder to adapt to without retraining from scratch.
- If the model only labels specific data types, it can introduce bias. This can result in a model that is optimized for those particular data types but may not perform well when faced with new data.
- The effectiveness of the approach may vary depending on the streaming platform and its limitations, which can restrict its usefulness.

Overall, stream-based selective sampling is an efficient approach when low storage and real-time response are critical. It works well when the stream distribution is relatively stable. If the stream changes over time, pool-based sampling may be more effective since earlier points can be re-analyzed.

Pool-based sampling

In the context of **pool-based sampling**, the active learner is given access to a large collection of unlabeled data points that remain static over time. The data points in that scenario are usually acquired from an existing unlabeled dataset or a labeled dataset where the labels are temporarily hidden. They can also be collected by scraping public sources.

Active learning selects data points from a static data pool and sends them to the oracle for labeling. Unlike the stream-based sampling scenario, none of the data points are discarded.

Figure 1.4 depicts a pool-based sampling workflow:

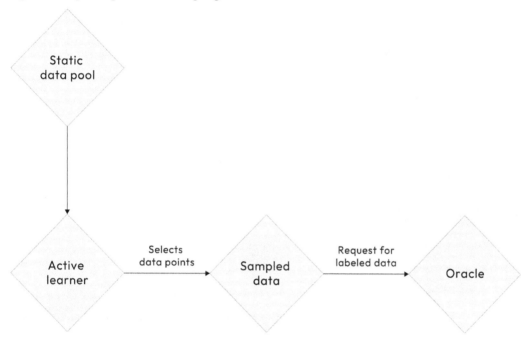

Figure 1.4 – Pool-based sampling workflow

The static pool serves as a dataset from which the learner can repeatedly draw samples, with the aim of acquiring the most informative labeled examples. By tapping into this pool, the learner can explore and extract valuable insights that contribute to the learning process. Through multiple iterations of sampling, the learner gains a deeper understanding and improves their ability to make informed decisions.

The pool is designed to provide users with the utmost flexibility, enabling them to query any point within the pool at any given time. This feature allows for seamless access to data points, ensuring convenience and versatility in the querying process. The size of the pool is determined based on computational constraints, with common sizes ranging from 10,000 to 1,000,000 data points. The choice of pool size depends on various factors, such as the computational resources available and the specific requirements of the model being used.

It is important to emphasize that throughout the iterative process, the pool remains fixed. The model continuously queries and selects the most valuable points from the pool, optimizing its performance and refining its results. This dynamic interplay between the pool and the model is essential in achieving optimal efficiency and accuracy in data analysis.

By maintaining a fixed pool size while iteratively querying for valuable points, the model ensures that it can adapt and evolve based on the changing needs of the analysis. This iterative approach allows the model to continuously refine its understanding and improve its predictions, leading to more insightful and accurate results.

For example, potential pool datasets could include the following:

- A database table with many unlabeled rows
- A collection of images, audio clips, or documents
- An existing ML dataset with the labels temporarily removed

Pool-based sampling offers several advantages, such as the following:

- Maximum flexibility in sampling. Any point can be queried multiple times
- The sampling strategy can be adjusted and improved over multiple iterations
- The ability to re-query points and fine-tune over time as the model changes

There are a few challenges as well:

- It requires sufficient storage for the full unlabeled pool dataset
- It is computationally intensive to search large, high-dimensional data pools for optimal queries
- The pool does not adapt over time in the way that a live data stream does.
- The model's accuracy depends on the selection method used to identify the most informative sample, which can reduce the model's accuracy

Overall, pool-based sampling provides the most practical active learning solution for many real-world applications. With sufficient storage and computation, it offers total flexibility in iterative querying. Stream-based sampling can complement in cases where real-time performance is critical.

Having explored the three different types of active ML scenarios, we can now assess how they differ from traditional passive learning methods.

Comparing active and passive learning

In traditional passive machine learning, models are trained on fixed and pre-existing labeled datasets, which are carefully assembled to include both data points and their respective ground truth labels. The model then goes through the dataset once, without any iteration or interaction, and learns the patterns and relationships between the features and labels. This is the passive learning approach. It's important to note that the model only trains on the finite data it is provided and cannot actively seek out new information or modify its training based on new inputs. Moreover, the labeled datasets required for a passive learning approach come at a cost.

There are several reasons why labeling is expensive in traditional machine learning:

- **Manual labeling requires experts**: Accurately labeling data often demands the expertise of domain specialists such as doctors or ecologists. However, their time is limited and valuable, making their involvement expensive.

- **Time-consuming process**: Manually labeling data such as images, audio clips, or text is a slow and tedious task that does not scale well. It can take minutes to hours to accurately label a single data point. While several annotation platforms integrate features and tools to make the labeling process smoother and faster, it still remains slow.

- **Annotation errors**: Some labels may be of lower quality due to overworked, rushed, or non-expert labelers. These incorrect and noisy labels can have a negative impact on the performance of models. To prevent this, additional oversight and one or more reviewing steps are often necessary.

- **Accumulating labeling costs**: When the cost per hour of labeling is multiplied by the number of examples needed, the overall expenses for data annotation can quickly become prohibitive, especially if several reviewing steps are needed. Modern deep learning models often require a large number of labeled examples, which can be very expensive.

- **Expanding model capabilities**: As new cases emerge, there is a constant need to acquire new labeled data. Continuously labeling evolving data poses a challenge.

All these reasons make passive labeling an expensive bottleneck. Minimizing these costs is crucial for developing scalable and accurate AI systems.

Active learning, on the other hand, takes an interactive and iterative approach. Instead of receiving a predefined labeled dataset, an active learning model dynamically chooses which data points it wants to be labeled. It analyzes a pool of unlabeled data and intelligently selects the most useful points to query an oracle for labels. The newly labeled data is then incorporated into its training set.

This introduces a feedback loop between data sampling, human labeling, and model training. The model guides its own learning by acquiring new training data specifically tailored to improve its weaknesses. Human effort is focused only on the most informative examples through selective sampling:

Characteristic	Passive Learning	Active Learning
Data Usage	Uses all available data at once	Selects the most informative data points
Learning Style	Learns from the entire dataset without asking queries	Asks queries (labels for instances) to learn better
Model Updating	The model is not updated unless new data is provided	The model actively updates itself by querying new data
Efficiency	Less efficient as it might learn from irrelevant data	More efficient as it learns from the most relevant data

Figure 1.5 – Passive learning and active learning – a comparison

One key advantage of active learning is that it reduces the total amount of labeled data required. Passive learners often need vast amounts of labeled examples to achieve desired performance, which can be costly and time-consuming to collect and prepare. Active learning minimizes this upfront labeling effort by acquiring only the examples that provide the maximum information value.

Furthermore, active learning systems can adapt and adjust over multiple iterations of querying. The model can change its sampling strategy based on previous rounds, re-query certain examples, or increase focus on areas where it is weakest. In contrast, passive learning involves a static dataset without room for adjustment.

Overall, active learning provides critical benefits of reduced labeling costs and flexible, adaptive training. By steering its own data collection, Active ML achieves higher predictive performance with significantly less reliance on vast labeled datasets.

Summary

In this introductory chapter, we covered the fundamentals of active ML and how it contrasts with passive learning approaches.

You learned what active learning is and its goal of maximizing predictive performance with fewer labeled training examples. We discussed the core components of an active learning system: the unlabeled data pool, query strategy, machine learning model, and the oracle labeler.

You now understand the difference between membership query synthesis, stream-based sampling, and pool-based sampling scenarios. We compared active and passive learning, highlighting the benefits of an interactive, iterative approach in active learning.

Importantly, you now know that active learning can produce models with equal or greater accuracy while requiring far less labeled training data. This is critical for reducing the costs of modeling, as labeling is often the most expensive component.

The skills you gained in this introduction will equip you to determine when active learning is appropriate for a problem. You can now correctly select the right components when implementing an active learning system.

Now that we have covered the fundamentals of active learning, query scenarios, and applications, the next step is to dive into specific query strategies. In the next chapter, we will explore frameworks for designing effective queries to identify the most valuable data points to label.

2

Designing Query Strategy Frameworks

Query strategies act as the engine that drives active ML and determines which data points get selected for labeling. In this chapter, we aim to provide a comprehensive and detailed explanation of the most widely used and highly effective query strategy frameworks that are employed in active ML. These frameworks play a crucial role in the field of active ML, aiding in selecting informative and representative data points for labeling. The strategies that we will delve into include uncertainty sampling, query-by-committee, **expected model change** (EMC), **expected error reduction** (EER), and density-weighted methods. By thoroughly understanding these frameworks and the underlying principles, you can make informed decisions when designing and implementing active ML algorithms.

In this chapter, you will gain skills that will equip you to design and deploy query strategies that extract maximum value from labeling efforts. You will gain intuition for matching strategies to datasets and use cases when building active ML systems.

We will cover the following topics:

- Exploring uncertainty sampling methods
- Understanding query-by-committee approaches
- Labeling with EMC sampling
- Sampling with EER
- Understanding density-weighted sampling methods

Technical requirements

For the code examples demonstrated in this chapter, we have used Python 3.9.6 with the following packages:

- `numpy` (version 1.23.5)
- `scikit-learn` (version 1.2.2)
- `matplotlib` (version 3.7.1)

Exploring uncertainty sampling methods

Uncertainty sampling refers to querying data points for which the model is least certain about their prediction. These are samples the model finds most ambiguous and cannot confidently label on its own. Getting these high-uncertainty points labeled allows the model to clarify where its knowledge is lacking.

In uncertainty sampling, the active ML system queries instances for which the current model's predictions exhibit *high uncertainty*. The goal is to select data points that are *near the decision boundary* between classes. Labeling these ambiguous examples helps the model gain confidence in areas where its knowledge is weakest.

Uncertainty sampling methods select data points close to the **decision boundary** because points near this boundary exhibit the highest prediction ambiguity. The decision boundary is defined as the point where the model shows the most uncertainty in distinguishing between different classes for a given input. Points on the boundary represent the most ambiguous, uncertain cases for a model.

Figure 2.1 illustrates the difference between uncertainty sampling and random sampling:

Figure 2.1 – Uncertainty sampling versus random sampling

For data points that are located far away from the decision boundary (*Figure 2.1*) within a class region (labeled as A or B), the model will exhibit a high level of confidence in assigning them to that class (for example, >95%). These points are considered certain and will not be selected when employing uncertainty sampling. However, there is a possibility that some of these points may be chosen when using random sampling. For data points that are extremely close to or directly on the decision boundary, the model will struggle to distinguish between the classes. The predicted class probabilities will be more evenly distributed, with the top predictions being very close to each other. Therefore, these points are considered uncertain and will be selected when using uncertainty sampling. These important data points might have been overlooked when using random sampling. As a result, the distance to the boundary correlates to uncertainty – the closest points will have the lowest max confidence, the smallest margin between top classes, and the highest entropy over the class probabilities.

Therefore, by selecting points based on metrics such as low confidence, low margin, and high entropy, uncertainty sampling queries the instances nearest to the decision boundary. We will discuss these metrics in detail in the upcoming sections of this chapter. Labeling these provides information to help clarify class regions and refine the boundary. The model is unlikely to gain much information from examples it can already predict correctly with high confidence. However, querying data points that the model is very uncertain about directly provides useful information about its gaps. Uncertainty sampling takes advantage of this by targeting points with high prediction ambiguity.

For example, an image classifier's least confident predictions likely correspond to challenging out-of-distribution examples that traditional sampling would miss. By querying these unusual cases for labels, the model rapidly improves at classifying edge cases. Now, let's discuss some of the common methods that are used for uncertainty sampling.

First, we will talk about **least-confidence sampling**, where the data points are ranked according to their least-confidence score. This score is obtained by subtracting the most confident prediction label for each item from 1, which represents 100% confidence. To facilitate understanding, it is beneficial to convert the uncertainty scores into a range of 0-1, where 1 signifies the highest level of uncertainty. The magnitude of the score that's assigned to each data point lies in its association with the uncertainty of the model's prediction. Consequently, data samples with the highest least-confident scores should be given priority for annotation.

The most informative sample, x, can be computed as follows:

$$x_{LC}^* = \underset{x}{\mathrm{argmax}}\left(1 - P_\theta(\hat{y}|x)\right)$$

Here, we have the following:

$$\hat{y} = \underset{x}{\mathrm{argmax}}\left(P_\theta(y|x)\right)$$

For instance, let's say we have a model that classifies samples into three different classes. Now, we are trying to rank two samples using least-confidence sampling. The predicted probabilities of the two samples are [0.05, 0.85, 0.10] for sample 1 and [0.35, 0.15, 0.50] for sample 2. Let's find out which sample is the most informative when using the least-confidence sampling method by using the following Python code:

```python
import numpy as np
# Model's probabilities of samples 1 and 2 for the 3 classes
probs_sample_1 = np.array([0.05, 0.85, 0.10])
probs_sample_2 = np.array([0.35, 0.15, 0.50])

def least_confident_score(predicted_probs):
    return 1 - predicted_probs[np.argmax(predicted_probs)]

LC_samples_scores = np.array(
    [least_confident_score(probs_sample_1),
    least_confident_score(probs_sample_2)])
print(f'Least confident score for sample 1 is:
    {LC_samples_scores[0]}')
print(f'Least confident score for sample 2 is:
    {LC_samples_scores[1]}')
most_informative_sample = np.argmax(LC_samples_scores)
print(f'The most informative sample is sample
    {most_informative_sample+1}')
```

The output of the preceding code snippet is as follows:

```
Least confident score for sample 1 is: 0.15000000000000002
Least confident score for sample 2 is: 0.5
```

Thus, the most informative sample is sample 2.

In this case, we can see that sample 2 is chosen when using the least-confidence sampling approach because the model's predictions were the least confident for that sample.

Next, we will discuss **margin sampling**. This method is designed to identify and select data points that have the smallest disparity in probability between the top two predicted classes. By focusing on data points with minimal margin between classes, we can effectively prioritize the annotation of data samples that result in a higher level of confusion for the model. Therefore, the model's level of uncertainty is higher when it encounters data points with a lower margin score, making them ideal candidates for annotation. The formula to calculate the score of the most informative data point with the margin sampling method is as follows:

$$x_M^* = \underset{x}{\operatorname{argmin}} \left(P_\theta(\hat{y}_{max1}|x) - P_\theta(\hat{y}_{max2}|x) \right)$$

Let's use the samples from our previous example again:

```python
import numpy as np

# Model's probabilities of sample 1 and 2 for the 3 classes
probs_sample_1 = np.array([0.05, 0.85, 0.10])
probs_sample_2 = np.array([0.35, 0.15, 0.50])

def margin_score(predicted_probs):
    predicted_probs_max_1 = np.sort(predicted_probs)[-1]
    predicted_probs_max_2 = np.sort(predicted_probs)[-2]
    margin_score = predicted_probs_max_1 - predicted_probs_max_2
    return margin_score

# For sample 1
margin_score_sample_1 = margin_score(probs_sample_1)
print(f'The margin score of sample 1 is: {margin_score_sample_1}')

# For sample 2
margin_score_sample_2 = margin_score(probs_sample_2)
print(f'The margin score of sample 2 is: {margin_score_sample_2}')

margin_scores = np.array([margin_score_sample_1,
    margin_score_sample_2])

most_informative_sample = np.argmin(margin_scores)
print(f'The most informative sample is sample
    {most_informative_sample+1}')
```

The output of the preceding script is as follows:

```
The margin score of sample 1 is: 0.75
The margin score of sample 2 is: 0.15000000000000002
The most informative sample is sample 2
```

With the margin sampling method, sample 2 is selected as well because it has the smallest disparity in probability between the top two predicted classes.

In the **ratio of confidence** method, the data points that have the smallest ratio between the probability of the top predicted class and the probability of the second most likely class are selected. This targets examples where the model's top two predictions are closest in likelihood. A lower ratio indicates that the model is less confident in the top class relative to the second class. By querying points with the minimum ratio between the top two class probabilities, this technique focuses on cases where the model is nearly equivocal between two classes. Getting these boundary points labeled will push the model to gain greater confidence in the true class. A lower ratio means higher ambiguity, so the ratio of confidence sampling finds points where the model is most unsure of which class is correct.

We can calculate the score of the most informative data point using the ratio of confidence sampling method via the following equation:

$$x_R^* = \underset{x}{\operatorname{argmin}} \left(\frac{P_\theta(\hat{y}_{max1}|x)}{P_\theta(\hat{y}_{max2}|x)} \right)$$

Once again, we'll utilize the samples that we used previously for this method:

```
import numpy as np

# Model's probabilities of sample 1 and 2 for the 3 classes
probs_sample_1 = np.array([0.05, 0.85, 0.10])
probs_sample_2 = np.array([0.35, 0.15, 0.50])

def ratio_score(predicted_probs):
    predicted_probs_max_1 = np.sort(predicted_probs)[-1]
    predicted_probs_max_2 = np.sort(predicted_probs)[-2]
    margin_score = predicted_probs_max_1 / predicted_probs_max_2
    return margin_score

# For sample 1
ratio_score_sample_1 = ratio_score(probs_sample_1)
print(f'The ratio score of sample 1 is: {ratio_score_sample_1}')

# For sample 2
ratio_score_sample_2 = ratio_score(probs_sample_2)
print(f'The ratio score of sample 2 is: {ratio_score_sample_2}')
margin_scores = np.array([ratio_score_sample_1, ratio_score_sample_2])
most_informative_sample = np.argmin(margin_scores)
print(f'The most informative sample is sample
    {most_informative_sample+1}')
```

The output of this script is as follows:

```
The ratio score of sample 1 is: 8.5
The ratio score of sample 2 is: 1.4285714285714286
The most informative sample is sample 2
```

So, sample 2 is selected when using the ratio of confidence sampling method as it has the smallest ratio between the probability of the top predicted class and the probability of the second most likely class.

Another method is **entropy sampling**. This method selects data points that have the highest entropy across the probability distribution over classes. Entropy represents the overall uncertainty in the predicted class probabilities. Higher entropy means the model is more uncertain, with a more uniform probability spread over classes. Lower entropy indicates confidence, with probability concentrated on one class.

By querying points with maximum entropy, this technique targets instances where the model's predicted class probabilities are most evenly distributed. These highly uncertain points provide the most information gain since the model cannot strongly favor one class – its predictions are maximally unsure. Getting these high entropy points labeled enables the model to gain more confidence in areas in which it is the most uncertain. Overall, entropy sampling finds points with the highest total ambiguity. The formula to calculate the score of the most informative data point with the entropy sampling method is as follows:

$$x_H^* = \underset{x}{\mathrm{argmax}} \left(-\sum_i P_\theta(y_i|x) \log \left(P_\theta(y_i|x) \right) \right)$$

Let's use our sample examples again with this method:

```python
import numpy as np

# Model's probabilities of sample 1 and 2 for the 3 classes
probs_sample_1 = np.array([0.05, 0.85, 0.10])
probs_sample_2 = np.array([0.35, 0.15, 0.50])

def entropy_score(predicted_probs):
    return -np.multiply(predicted_probs, \
        np.nan_to_num(np.log2(predicted_probs))).sum()

# For sample 1
entropy_score_sample_1 = entropy_score(probs_sample_1)
print(f'The margin score of sample 1 is: {entropy_score_sample_1}')

# For sample 2
entropy_score_sample_2 = entropy_score(probs_sample_2)
print(f'The margin score of sample 2 is: {entropy_score_sample_2}')

entropy_scores = np.array([entropy_score_sample_1, \
    entropy_score_sample_2])

most_informative_sample = np.argmax(entropy_scores)
print(f'The most informative sample is sample
    {most_informative_sample+1}')
```

This script outputs the following results:

```
The margin score of sample 1 is: 0.747584679824574
The margin score of sample 2 is: 1.4406454496153462
The most informative sample is sample 2.
```

Using entropy sampling, sample 2 was chosen as it has the highest entropy across the probability distribution over classes.

These common uncertainty sampling techniques provide simple but effective strategies to identify highly ambiguous points to query.

Now, let's explore the key benefits that uncertainty sampling provides for active ML:

- Uncertainty sampling is a conceptually intuitive query strategy that is efficient to compute. Metrics such as confidence, margin, ratio, and entropy have clear uncertainty interpretations and can be calculated quickly.

- It actively enhances model confidence in areas where it is uncertain, expanding knowledge boundaries. For example, a sentiment classifier can gain more certainty on ambiguous reviews containing rare phrases by querying the most uncertain cases for their true sentiment.

- Uncertainty sampling is widely applicable across classification tasks and model types such as **support vector machines** (**SVMs**), logistic regression, random forests, and **neural networks** (**NNs**). Uncertainty applies broadly to classification tasks.

- Uncertainty sampling is useful for anomaly detection by finding ambiguous outliers the model cannot explain. Uncertainty highlights unusual cases.

- It can identify labeling errors by seeking points with inconsistent predictions between models. High uncertainty may indicate noisy data.

Overall, uncertainty sampling is a highly effective and versatile active ML method. It can be used in various domains and is intuitive and efficient. It helps expand a model's capabilities and discover unknown points. Whether it's used for classification, regression, or other ML tasks, uncertainty sampling consistently improves model performance. By selecting uncertain data points for annotation, the model learns from informative examples and improves predictions. It has proven useful in natural language processing, computer vision, and data mining. Uncertainty sampling actively acquires new knowledge and enhances ML models. While uncertainty sampling focuses on points the model is individually unsure of, query-by-committee approaches aim to add diversity by identifying points where an ensemble of models disagrees. We will discuss query-by-committee approaches in the next section.

Understanding query-by-committee approaches

Query-by-committee aims to add diversity by querying points where an ensemble of models disagrees the most. Different models will disagree where the data is most uncertain or ambiguous.

In the query-by-committee approach, a group of models is trained using a labeled set of data. By doing so, the ensemble can work together and provide a more robust and accurate prediction.

One interesting aspect of this approach is that it identifies the data point that causes the most disagreement among the ensemble members. This data point is then chosen to be queried to obtain a label.

The reason why this method works well is because different models tend to have the most disagreement on difficult and boundary examples, as depicted in *Figure 2.2*. These are the instances where there is ambiguity or uncertainty, and by focusing on these points of maximal disagreement, the ensemble can gain consensus and make more confident predictions:

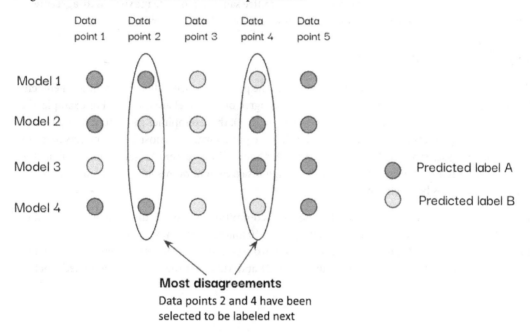

Figure 2.2 – Query-by-committee sampling with five unlabeled data points

Figure 2.2 reveals a disagreement between models 1 and 4, as opposed to models 2 and 3, regarding data point 2. A similar pattern can be observed with data point 4. Therefore, data points 2 and 4 have been chosen to be sent to the oracle for labeling.

Query-by-committee is a widely used and effective active ML strategy that addresses the limitations of uncertainty sampling. While uncertainty sampling can be biased toward the current learner and may overlook crucial examples that are not within its estimator's focus, query-by-committee overcomes these challenges. This approach involves maintaining multiple hypotheses simultaneously and selecting queries that lead to disagreements among these hypotheses. By doing so, it ensures a more comprehensive and diverse exploration of the data, ultimately enhancing the learning process. For instance, a committee of image classifiers may heavily disagree on ambiguous images that traditional sampling fails to capture. By querying labels for images with maximal disagreement, such as varied predictions for an unusual object, the committee collectively improves.

Some of the common techniques for query-by-committee sampling include **maximum disagreement**, **vote entropy**, and **average KL divergence**, all of which we will discuss now.

Maximum disagreement

This simple approach looks at direct disagreement in the predicted labels between committee members. The data points where most ensemble members disagree on the label are queried. For example, if a three-model committee's label votes for a point are (1, 2, 3), this exemplifies maximum disagreement as each model predicts a different class. Querying the points with the most label conflicts helps us focus only on cases that divide the committee. Maximum disagreement target instances create the largest rifts within the ensemble. Getting these high disagreement points labeled will aim to resolve the core differences between models.

Let's explore a numerical example of the query-by-committee maximum disagreement method in active ML. For this example, we will consider a pool of 10 unlabeled data points, as shown in *Figure 2.3*, that we want to label to train a classifier. We create two committee members (models) called M1 and M2. We evaluate each unlabeled data point using M1 and M2 to get the following predicted labels:

Data Point	M1 Predicted Label	M2 Predicted Label
1	0	1
2	1	1
3	0	0
4	1	0
5	0	1
6	1	1
7	0	0
8	1	0
9	0	1
10	1	1

Figure 2.3 – A numerical example to illustrate the query-by-committee maximum disagreement method

Then, we select the data point with the maximum disagreement between the two committee members. Here, data points 1, 4, 5, 8, and 9 have different predicted labels by M1 and M2. We select one of these points, say point 4, to query the true label from an oracle. We then add the newly labeled point to retrain the committee members.

We can do this with a simple Python script:

```python
import numpy as np

# Predicted labels from 2 committee members
y1 = np.array([0, 1, 0, 1, 0, 1, 0, 1, 0, 1])
y2 = np.array([1, 1, 0, 0, 1, 1, 0, 0, 1, 1])

# Calculate disagreement
disagreement = np.abs(y1 - y2)

# Find index of point with max disagreement
query_index = np.argmax(disagreement)

print(f"Data point {query_index+1} selected with maximum
disagreement")
```

This returns the following output:

```
Data point 1 selected with maximum disagreement
```

This process is then repeated, querying points with maximum disagreement in labels predicted by the committee, until we reach sufficient performance. The most informative points surface through the maximum disagreement of the committee members.

Vote entropy

This technique calculates the entropy over the label votes from each model in the ensemble committee. **Entropy** represents the overall uncertainty, where higher entropy means the models have a wider spread of predictions. Lower entropy indicates the models largely agree on the label. Querying the data points with maximum entropy in the vote distribution helps target the instances where the committee displays the highest collective uncertainty and disagreement. Getting these maximally entropic points labeled will push the ensemble toward greater consensus. Overall, vote entropy identifies cases that divide the committee the most, focusing labeling on their disagreements. If we go back to using a numerical example to better understand how the query-by-committee vote entropy method works, we can once again use a pool of 10 unlabeled data points, as shown in *Figure 2.4*, and a committee of two models, M1 and M2. We get the following predicted probabilities for each class on the data points:

Data Point	M1 Prob Class 0	M1 Prob Class 1	M2 Prob Class 0	M2 Prob Class 1
1	0.6	0.4	0.3	0.7
2	0.2	0.8	0.1	0.9
3	0.8	0.2	0.9	0.1
4	0.4	0.6	0.7	0.3
5	0.7	0.3	0.4	0.6
6	0.2	0.8	0.1	0.9
7	0.9	0.1	0.8	0.2
8	0.5	0.5	0.4	0.6
9	0.3	0.7	0.6	0.4
10	0.1	0.9	0.2	0.8

Figure 2.4 – A numerical example to illustrate the query-by-committee vote entropy method

We calculate the vote entropy for each point as follows:

$$H(x) = - \sum_i P(y|x)\log(y|x)$$

Here, $P(y|x)$ is averaged over the committee members.

The probabilities from the committee members are averaged when calculating the vote entropy because we want to measure the total uncertainty or disagreement of the entire committee on a data point. By averaging, we essentially get the *vote* of the full committee on the probabilities of each class, rather than just considering individual members' predictions. This allows us to select the data points where the committee has the most uncertainty or disagrees the most with its predictions:

Data Point	M1 Prob Class 0	M1 Prob Class 1	M2 Prob Class 0	M2 Prob Class 1	Average Class 0	Average Class 1	Entropy
1	0.6	0.4	0.3	0.7	0.45	0.55	-0.55log(0.55) - 0.45log(0.45) = 0.99
2	0.2	0.8	0.1	0.9	0.15	0.85	-0.15log(0.15) - 0.85log(0.85) = 0.61
3	0.8	0.2	0.9	0.1	0.85	0.15	-0.85log(0.85) - 0.15log(0.15) = 0.61
4	0.4	0.6	0.7	0.3	0.55	0.45	-0.55log(0.55) - 0.45log(0.45) = 0.99
5	0.7	0.3	0.4	0.6	0.55	0.45	-0.55log(0.55) - 0.45log(0.45) = 0.99
6	0.2	0.8	0.1	0.9	0.15	0.85	-0.15log(0.15) - 0.85log(0.85) = 0.61
7	0.9	0.1	0.8	0.2	0.85	0.15	-0.85log(0.85) - 0.15log(0.15) = 0.61
8	0.5	0.5	0.4	0.6	0.45	0.55	-0.45log(0.45) - 0.55log(0.55) = 0.99
9	0.3	0.7	0.6	0.4	0.45	0.55	-0.45log(0.45) - 0.55log(0.55) = 0.99
10	0.1	0.9	0.2	0.8	0.15	0.85	-0.15log(0.15) - 0.85log(0.85) = 0.61

Figure 2.5 – A numerical example to illustrate the query-by-committee vote
entropy method with averages per class and entropy calculated

The points with maximum entropy will have the most disagreement among models. In *Figure 2.5*, points 1, 4, 5, 8, and 9 have the highest entropy, so we query their labels. The next step would be to retrain the models and repeat the process.

We can write this with some Python code as well:

```
import numpy as np

p1 = np.array([[0.6, 0.4], [0.2, 0.8], [0.8, 0.2], [0.4, 0.6], [0.7,
0.3],
                [0.2, 0.8], [0.9, 0.1], [0.5, 0.5], [0.3, 0.7], [0.1,
```

```
0.9]])

p2 = np.array([[0.3, 0.7], [0.1, 0.9], [0.9, 0.1], [0.7, 0.3], [0.4,
0.6],
                [0.1, 0.9], [0.8, 0.2], [0.4, 0.6], [0.6, 0.4], [0.2,
0.8]])

# Average probabilities per class
p_class0 = (p1[:, 0] + p2[:, 0]) / 2
p_class1 = (p1[:, 1] + p2[:, 1]) / 2

p_avg = np.concatenate((p_class0.reshape(-1, 1), \
    p_class1.reshape(-1, 1)), axis=1)

# Calculate entropy
H = -np.sum(p_avg * np.log2(p_avg), axis=1)

query_index = np.argmax(H)
print(f"Data point {query_index+1} selected with maximum entropy of
{H[query_index]}")
```

The output of this script is as follows:

```
Data point 1 selected with maximum entropy of 0.9927744539878083
```

Next, we will move our focus to computing predictions using the KL divergence method.

Average KL divergence

This method measures the **Kullback-Leibler divergence** (**KL divergence**) between each committee member's predicted label distribution and the average predicted distribution across all members.

KL divergence is defined as follows:

$$D_{KL}\left(P\middle\|Q\right) = -\sum_{x\in X}P\left(x\right)\log\left(\frac{Q(x)}{P(x)}\right)$$

Here, P and Q are two probability distributions.

The data points with the highest average KL divergence are then queried. A higher KL divergence indicates a larger difference between a model's predictions and the committee consensus. Querying points with maximum divergence targets instances where individual models strongly disagree with the overall ensemble. Labeling these high-divergence points will bring the individual models closer to the committee average. Average KL divergence identifies cases with outlying model predictions to focus labeling on reconciliation. Let's take a look at our numerical example for the query-by-committee average KL divergence method. Again, we're using the pool of 10 unlabeled data points, as shown in

Figure 2.6, and a committee of two models, M1 and M2. We get the predicted class probabilities on each data point from M1 and M2 and calculate the KL divergence between M1's and M2's predictions for each point:

Data Point	M1 Prob Class 0	M1 Prob Class 1	M2 Prob Class 0	M2 Prob Class 1	KL(M1||M2)	KL(M2||M1)	Average KL Divergence
1	0.6	0.4	0.3	0.7	0.19	0.18	0.19
2	0.2	0.8	0.1	0.9	0.04	0.04	0.04
3	0.8	0.2	0.9	0.1	0.04	0.04	0.04
4	0.4	0.6	0.7	0.3	0.19	0.18	0.19
5	0.7	0.3	0.4	0.6	0.18	0.19	0.19
6	0.2	0.8	0.1	0.9	0.04	0.04	0.04
7	0.9	0.1	0.8	0.2	0.04	0.04	0.04
8	0.5	0.5	0.4	0.6	0.02	0.02	0.02
9	0.3	0.7	0.6	0.4	0.18	0.19	0.19
10	0.1	0.9	0.2	0.8	0.04	0.04	0.04

Figure 2.6 – A numerical example to illustrate the query-by-committee average KL divergence method

We average the KL divergence between M1 and M2, and M2 and M1. We calculate the KL divergence in both directions (KL(M1||M2) and KL(M2||M1)) – because KL divergence is asymmetric, it will give different values depending on the direction.

The KL divergence from M1 to M2, KL(M1||M2), measures how well M2's distribution approximates M1's. On the other hand, KL(M2||M1) measures how well M1's distribution approximates M2's.

In query-by-committee, we want to measure the total disagreement between the two committee members' distributions. Just using KL(M1||M2) or just using KL(M2||M1) will not capture the full divergence. By taking the average of KL(M1||M2) and KL(M2||M1), we get a symmetric measure of the total divergence between the two distributions. This gives a better indication of the overall disagreement between the two committee members on a data point.

Taking the average KL in both directions ensures we select the points with maximum mutual divergence between the two models' predictions. This surfaces the most informative points for labeling to resolve the committee's uncertainty. The point with maximum average KL divergence has the most disagreement. So, here, points 1, 4, 5, and 9 have the highest average KL divergence. We would then query these labels, retrain the models, and repeat the process.

We can write this with some Python code as well:

```
import numpy as np

p1 = np.array([[0.6, 0.4], [0.2, 0.8], [0.8, 0.2], [0.4, 0.6], [0.7,
0.3],
                [0.2, 0.8], [0.9, 0.1], [0.5, 0.5], [0.3, 0.7], [0.1,
0.9]])

p2 = np.array([[0.3, 0.7], [0.1, 0.9], [0.9, 0.1], [0.7, 0.3], [0.4,
0.6],
                [0.1, 0.9], [0.8, 0.2], [0.4, 0.6], [0.6, 0.4], [0.2,
0.8]])

KL1 = np.sum(p1 * np.log(p1 / p2), axis=1)
KL2 = np.sum(p2 * np.log(p2 / p1), axis=1)
avg_KL = (KL1 + KL2) / 2

print("KL(M1||M2):", KL1)
print("KL(M2||M1):", KL2)
print("Average KL:", avg_KL)

query_index = np.argmax(avg_KL)
print("\nData point", query_index+1, "selected with max average KL
of", avg_KL[query_index])
```

Here's the output we get:

```
KL(M1||M2): [0.19204199 0.04440301 0.04440301 0.19204199
0.1837869   0.04440301
0.03669001 0.020411   0.1837869   0.03669001]
KL(M2||M1): [0.1837869   0.03669001 0.03669001 0.1837869   0.19204199
0.03669001
0.04440301 0.02013551 0.19204199 0.04440301]
Average KL: [0.18791445 0.04054651 0.04054651 0.18791445 0.18791445
0.04054651
0.04054651 0.02027326 0.18791445 0.04054651]

Data point 1 selected with max average KL of 0.18791444527430518
```

Upon exploring different methods that are used to perform query-by-committee sampling, we've noticed that it can be quite computationally intensive. Indeed, as shown in *Figure 2.7*, the query-by-committee technique is an iterative approach that requires retraining the models from the committee every time new labeled data is added to the training set:

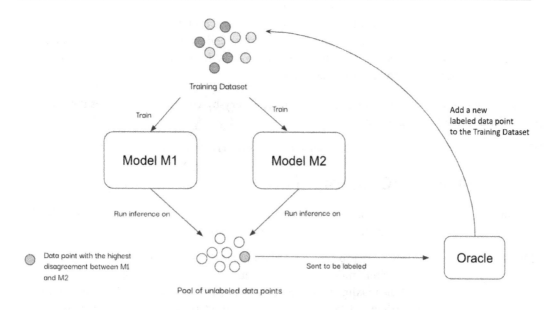

Figure 2.7 – The iteration process in the query-by-committee sampling technique

In conclusion, this technique is designed to identify informative query points by quantifying the level of disagreement among the ensemble models and offers several key advantages:

- It promotes diversity by finding points that various models interpret differently. The techniques can effectively prioritize query points that are likely to provide valuable information, thus improving the overall quality of the query-based learning process.

- It encourages exploration by actively seeking out query points that are less predictable or commonly known, allowing for a more comprehensive understanding of the dataset.

- It provides the ability to construct committees with an array of distinct models such as SVMs, NNs, and many others. This versatility allows for a diverse range of strategies and approaches to be employed when making important decisions. By leveraging these various models, you can gain deeper insights and improve the overall performance of your committee. The query-by-committee approach differs from traditional techniques such as bagging and boosting. Its main objective is to choose the most informative unlabeled data points for labeling and inclusion in the training set. On the other hand, traditional ensemble methods such as bagging and boosting focus on combining multiple models to enhance overall predictive performance. Indeed, query-by-committee methods calculate disagreement between committee members to find optimal queries for labeling, as we have seen previously. Traditional ensembles combine predictions through voting or averaging to produce a unified prediction.

- It is very useful in situations where the unlabeled data pool contains a limited representation of the underlying distribution. By combining the opinions and predictions of different committee members, query-by-committee methods can effectively address the challenges posed by poorly covered distributions in unlabeled data pools.

By leveraging the varying opinions of the committee, query-by-committee enhances the overall performance of the learning system.

We will now delve deeper into the implementation of EMC strategies and explore their potential benefits.

Labeling with EMC sampling

EMC aims to query points that will induce the greatest change in the current model when labeled and trained on. This focuses labeling on points with the highest expected impact.

EMC techniques involve selecting a specific data point to label and learn from to cause the most significant alteration to the current model's parameters and predictions. The core idea is to query the point that would impact the maximum change to the model's parameters if we knew its label. By carefully identifying this particular data point, the EMC method aims to maximize the impact on the model and improve its overall performance. The process involves assessing various factors and analyzing the potential effects of each data point, ultimately choosing the one that is expected to yield the most substantial changes to the model, as depicted in *Figure 2.8*. The goal is to enhance the model's accuracy and make it more effective in making predictions.

When we refer to querying points that lead to larger updates in the model targets, what we are discussing is identifying highly informative examples located in uncertain areas of the input space. These examples play a crucial role in influencing and enhancing the model's performance. By paying attention to these specific instances, we can gain deeper insights into the complexities and subtleties of the input space, resulting in a more thorough understanding and improved overall outcomes:

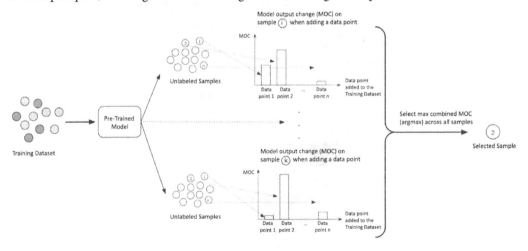

Figure 2.8 – EMC sampling

The initial model is trained using the training dataset. Then, the unlabeled samples are evaluated based on the changes in model outputs after including them in the training set. In *Figure 2.8*, the graphs show the resulting **model output change** (**MOC**) for three example samples. The sample that leads to the largest output change, when considering all data, is chosen to be labeled next.

In other words, in EMC sampling, the process begins by ranking the unlabeled examples. This ranking is determined by estimating the expected change that would occur in the model's predictions if each example were to be labeled. This estimation takes into account various factors and considerations, ultimately providing a basis for the prioritization of labeling.

This estimation is typically based on calculating the **expected gradient length** (**EGL**). The EGL method estimates the expected length of the gradient of the loss function if the model was trained on the newly labeled point. When training discriminative probabilistic models, gradient-based optimization is commonly used. To assess the *change* in the model, we can examine the size of the training gradient. This gradient refers to the vector that is employed to update the parameter values during the training process. In simpler terms, the learner should choose the instance, x_{EGL}^{*}, that, when labeled and included in the labeled dataset, ($\mathscr{L}$), would result in the greatest magnitude for the new training gradient:

$$x_{EGL}^{*} = \underset{x}{\mathrm{argmax}} \sum_{i} P(y_{i}|x;\theta) \left\| \nabla \ell \left(\mathscr{L} \cup \langle x, y_{i} \rangle; \theta \right) \right\|$$

Here, $\|.\|$ is the Euclidean norm of each resulting gradient vector, θ is the model parameters, x is an unlabeled point, y is the predicted label for x, and $\nabla \ell \left(\mathscr{L} \cup \langle x, y_{i} \rangle; \theta \right)$ is the new gradient that would be obtained by adding the training tuple, $\langle x, y \rangle$, to the labeled dataset, ($\mathscr{L}$). Data points that result in a longer expected gradient are prioritized for querying. A longer gradient indicates a greater expected change in the model parameters during training. By selecting points with high expected gradient length, the model focuses on samples that will highly influence the model once labeled. This targets points in uncertain regions that will have an outsized impact on updating model predictions. In short, EGL identifies data points that are likely to substantially reshape the decision boundary.

By employing this technique, the algorithm can pinpoint and identify the specific data points that are anticipated to yield substantial alterations in the model's predictions. The selected examples are subsequently sent for labeling as they are believed to possess the most value in terms of training the model effectively. Once designated, these informative samples are seamlessly integrated into the existing training data, thereby facilitating the necessary updates and improvements to the model's overall performance and accuracy.

There are several key advantages of the EMC method:

- Its ability to actively seek out influential and under-represented regions within the input space. This means that it can effectively identify areas that may have been overlooked or not given enough attention in a traditional modeling approach. Suppose we are training a model to predict housing prices. The input features are things such as square footage, number of bedrooms, location, and so on. Using a traditional modeling approach, we may collect a random sample of houses to train the model on. However, this could lead to certain neighborhoods or house styles being under-represented if they are less common. The EMC method would analyze the current model and identify areas where new training data would likely lead to the largest change in the model predictions. For example, it may find that adding more samples from older houses could better calibrate the model's understanding of how age affects price, or gathering data from a new suburban development that is under-represented could improve the performance of houses in that area. By actively seeking these influential regions, EMC can make the model more robust with fewer overall training examples. It reduces the risk of underfitting certain areas of the input space compared to passive or random data collection. It can help uncover hidden patterns or relationships that may not be immediately apparent, further enhancing the overall understanding of the dataset.

- It is compatible with probabilistic and kernel-based models. By leveraging the probabilistic nature of these models, the EMC method can provide insightful and accurate predictions. Additionally, its compatibility with kernel-based models allows for an enhanced understanding of complex data patterns and relationships. This combination of features makes the EMC method a powerful tool for analyzing and interpreting data in a wide range of domains.

- It allows for estimation without the need for full retraining at each step. This means that the process can be more efficient and less time-consuming as it eliminates the need to repeatedly train the model from scratch. Instead, the method enables model changes to be estimated by focusing on the expected changes in the model's parameters. By utilizing this approach, you can save valuable time and resources while still obtaining accurate and reliable estimations.

In summary, EMC queries aim to identify points with the highest potential impact on the model. It selects those with the maximum expected impact. This method is widely discussed in literature but not implemented in practice due to its high computational cost.

Next, we'll explore EER sampling. This technique reduces the model's error by selecting points that are expected to contribute the most to error reduction. By strategically sampling these points, we can improve overall model accuracy.

Sampling with EER

EER focuses on measuring the potential decrease in generalization error instead of the expected change in the model, as seen in the previous approach. The goal is to estimate the anticipated future error of a model by training it with the current labeled set and the remaining unlabeled samples. EER can be defined as follows:

$$E_{\hat{P}_{\mathscr{L}}} = \int_x L\big(P(y|x), \hat{P}(y|x)\big)P(x)$$

Here, $\mathscr{L}$ is the pool of paired labeled data, $P(x)P(y|x)$, and $\hat{P}_{\mathscr{L}}(y|x)$ is the estimated output distribution. L is a chosen loss function that measures the error between the true distribution, $P(y|x)$, and the learner's prediction, $\hat{P}_{\mathscr{L}}(y|x)$.

This involves selecting the instance that is expected to have the lowest future error (referred to as *risk*) for querying. This focuses active ML on reducing long-term generalization errors rather than just immediate training performance.

In other words, EER selects unlabeled data points that, when queried and learned from, are expected to significantly reduce the model's errors on new data points from the same distribution. By focusing on points that minimize future expected errors, as shown in *Figure 2.9*, EER aims to identify valuable training examples that will enhance the model's ability to generalize effectively. This technique targets high-value training examples that will improve the model's performance by minimizing incorrect predictions.

This approach helps prevent short-term overfitting by avoiding the inclusion of redundant similar examples and instead focusing on diverse edge cases that better span the feature space. For instance, in the case of an image classifier, the technique may prioritize the inclusion of diverse edge cases that capture a wide range of features rather than including redundant similar examples:

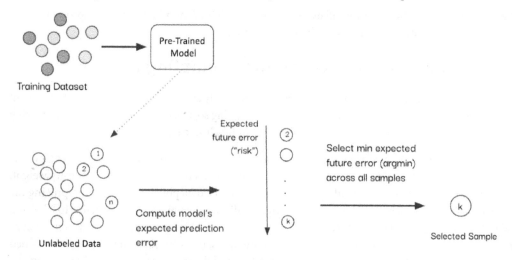

Figure 2.9 – EER sampling

Computing the expected model's prediction error can be done using various loss functions, such as the log loss, which is defined as $L = \sum_{y \in Y} P(y|x) \log \left(\widehat{P}_{\mathscr{L}}(y|x) \right)$, or the 0/1 loss, which is defined as $L = 1 - \max_{y \in Y} \widehat{P}_{\mathscr{L}}(y|x)$.

EER incurs a significant time cost due to the estimation of error reduction. To calculate the expected generalization error, the classifier must be re-optimized for each data point, considering its possible labels. Additionally, it is necessary to re-infer the labels of other data points. However, this technique offers a couple of key advantages:

- It allows direct optimization of the true objective of reducing the generalization error instead of solely focusing on improving training performance. By prioritizing the reduction of the generalization error, EER allows for more accurate and reliable predictions in real-world scenarios. This not only enhances the overall performance of the model but also ensures that it can effectively generalize to unseen data.

- It considers the impact on unseen data points, going beyond just the training set. By doing so, EER helps to mitigate overfitting, which is a common challenge in ML and statistical modeling. Overfitting occurs when a model performs exceedingly well on the training data but fails to generalize well to new, unseen data. EER tackles this issue head-on by incorporating a comprehensive evaluation of potential errors and their reduction. This ensures that the model's performance is not limited to the training set and instead extends to real-world scenarios, making it a valuable tool in data-driven decision-making.

EER is a predictive and robust query framework that focuses on maximally reducing the model's generalization error. Similar to the EMC method, the EER method is a topic of extensive discussion in literature. However, it has not been widely adopted in practical applications primarily because of the significant computational resources it demands.

The next sampling method that we will explore, density-weighted sampling, aims to improve diversity by selecting representative points from all density regions.

Understanding density-weighted sampling methods

Density-weighted methods are approaches that aim to carefully choose points that accurately represent the densities of their respective local neighborhoods. By doing so, these methods prioritize the labeling of diverse cluster centers, ensuring a comprehensive and inclusive representation of the data.

Density-weighted techniques are highly beneficial and effective when it comes to querying points. These techniques utilize a clever combination of an informativeness measure and a density weight. An **informativeness measure** provides a score of how useful a data point would be for improving the model if we queried its label. Higher informativeness indicates the point is more valuable to label and add to the training set. In this chapter, we have explored several informativeness measures, such as uncertainty and disagreement. In density-weighted methods, the informativeness score is combined with a density weight to ensure we select representative and diverse queries across different regions of the input space. This is done by assigning a weight to each data point based on both its density and its informativeness. Data points with higher informativeness and lower density will be given a higher weight, and will therefore be more likely to be selected for labeling. Points in dense clusters receive lower weights. The density and informativeness are combined through multiplicative, exponential, or additive formulations. This balances informativeness with density to achieve diversity.

The density weight represents the density of the local neighborhood surrounding each point, allowing for a more comprehensive and accurate sampling of points from different densities, as shown in *Figure 2.10*. This approach avoids the pitfall of solely focusing on dense clusters, which could result in redundant points. By taking into account the density weight, these techniques guarantee that the selected points effectively capture the overall distribution of the dataset. As a result, the obtained results are more meaningful and provide deeper insights into the data:

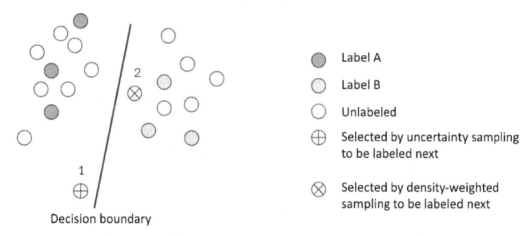

Figure 2.10 – Density-weighted sampling

In *Figure 2.10*, we can observe the significance of sample density in the active ML process. With instance 1 being positioned near the decision boundary, this makes it a prime candidate for being chosen as the most uncertain one. However, if we analyze the situation more closely, it becomes apparent that selecting instance 2 would be more advantageous in terms of enhancing the overall quality of the model. This is because instance 2 not only represents itself accurately but also acts as a representative for other instances within the data distribution. Therefore, its inclusion in the active ML process can lead to more comprehensive and reliable model improvements.

Implementing queries that would select instance 2 in the preceding example can be done with various density-weighted sampling methods, such as kNN density, **kernel density estimation (KDE)**, K-means clustering, and **maximum mean discrepancy (MMD)**.

Let's start with the imports and generating the dummy data:

```
import numpy as np
import matplotlib.pyplot as plt
from sklearn.neighbors import NearestNeighbors
from sklearn.neighbors import KernelDensity
from sklearn.cluster import KMeans
from sklearn.metrics.pairwise import pairwise_distances

# Generate sample 2D data
np.random.seed(1)
X = np.concatenate((np.random.randn(100, 2) + [2, 2],
                    np.random.randn(50, 2)))
```

Now, let's understand and apply different density-based techniques for our X sample data:

- **kNN density** calculates the local density around each data point using its *k-nearest neighbors*. The density is estimated by taking the inverse of the average distance to the k-closest points. Denser points have higher density, while isolated points have lower density. The estimated density is then used as a weight. When combined with informativeness criteria such as uncertainty, points in sparser neighborhoods get higher density weights, increasing their priority. kNN density weighting provides an efficient way to increase sample diversity and avoid over-sampling clusters when querying:

  ```
  # kNN density
  knn = NearestNeighbors(n_neighbors=5).fit(X)
  distances, _ = knn.kneighbors(X)
  knn_density = 1 / distances.sum(axis=1)
  ```

- **KDE** estimates the local density around each point using a kernel function centered on the point. Typically, a Gaussian kernel is used. The densities from the kernels of nearby points are summed to get the overall estimated density. As with kNN density, points in sparser regions will have lower kernel density compared to crowded areas. These density values can be used as weights when combined with informativeness criteria. Points in isolated clusters will be up-weighted, increasing their query priority. KDE provides a smooth, probabilistic estimate of local density, as opposed to the discrete clusters of kNN. It is more computationally expensive than kNN but can be implemented efficiently in high dimensions. KDE weighting focuses sampling on representative low-density points:

  ```
  # Kernel density estimation
  kde = KernelDensity(kernel='gaussian', bandwidth=0.2).fit(X)
  kde_dens = np.exp(kde.score_samples(X))
  ```

- **K-means density** clusters the unlabeled data points using k-means into k clusters. The size of each cluster indicates its density – smaller clusters correspond to sparser regions. This cluster density can be used as a weight when combined with informativeness criteria. Points in smaller, tighter clusters get increased weight, making them more likely to be queried. This balances sampling across varying densities. K-means provides a simple way to estimate density and identify representative points from all densities. It is fast and scales well to large datasets. One limitation is determining the number of clusters, k, upfront. K-means density weighting focuses active ML on diverse cases from all densities equally:

```
# K-means clustering
km = KMeans(n_clusters=5).fit(X)
km_density = 1 / pairwise_distances(X,
    km.cluster_centers_).sum(axis=1)
```

- **MMD** measures the *distance* between distributions to identify points in low-density regions. The MMD between a point's neighborhood distribution and the overall data distribution is calculated. A higher MMD indicates that the local region is very different from the overall distribution, so it is likely a low-density area. These MMD density scores are then used as weights when combined with informativeness measures. Points in sparse, isolated regions with high MMD get increased priority for querying. This results in balanced sampling across varying densities, thereby avoiding cluster oversampling. MMD provides a principled way to estimate density that captures useful nonlinear variations. MMD density weighting focuses active ML on representative low-density areas:

```
# Maximum Mean Discrepancy
mmd = pairwise_distances(X).mean()
mmd_density = 1 / pairwise_distances(X).sum(axis=1)
```

Now, let's visualize these density-weight sampling methods:

```
# Plot the density estimations
fig, axs = plt.subplots(2, 2, figsize=(12, 8))
axs[0, 0].scatter(X[:, 0], X[:, 1], c=knn_density)
axs[0, 0].set_title('kNN Density')

axs[0, 1].scatter(X[:, 0], X[:, 1], c=kde_dens)
axs[0, 1].set_title('Kernel Density')

axs[1, 0].scatter(X[:, 0], X[:, 1], c=km_density)
axs[1, 0].set_title('K-Means Density')

axs[1, 1].scatter(X[:, 0], X[:, 1], c=mmd_density)
axs[1, 1].set_title('Maximum mean discrepancy (MMD) Density')
```

```
fig.suptitle('Density-Weighted Sampling methods')
plt.show()
```

The resulting graph is presented in *Figure 2.11*:

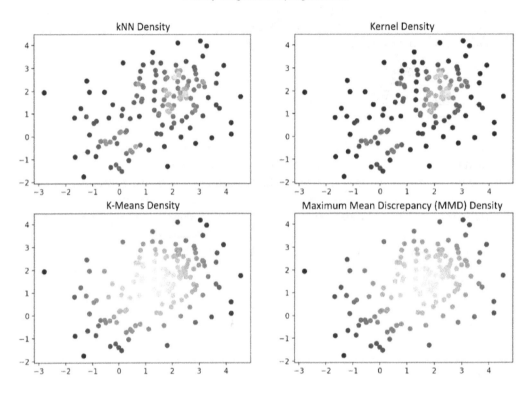

Figure 2.11 – A comparison of different density-weighted sampling methods

Density-weighted sampling methods, including the ones mentioned previously, offer diverse advantages:

- They can help improve the performance of the ML model by selecting samples that are more likely to be informative. This is because samples that are in high-density regions of the data are more likely to be representative of the underlying distribution and therefore more likely to be informative for the model.

- They help reduce the number of labeled samples needed to train the model. This is because density-weighted sampling can help focus the labeling effort on the most informative samples, which can lead to faster convergence of the model.

- They can be used with any type of data. Density-weighted sampling does not make any assumptions about the data distribution, so it can be used with any type of data, including structured and unstructured data.

To conclude, density weighting, which is a technique that's used to increase the diversity and coverage of samples, offers an effective and efficient approach. By assigning weights to each sample based on their density, this method ensures that the resulting sample set represents the underlying population more accurately. With this approach, you can obtain a more comprehensive understanding of the data, allowing for better decision-making and analysis. Overall, density weighting is a valuable tool in research and statistical analysis, allowing you to highlight hidden patterns and trends that might otherwise be overlooked.

Now that we have discussed several query strategies, let's compare them to understand how they fare against each other:

Method	Metric	Description	Advantages	Disadvantages	Requires Retraining
Uncertainty Sampling	- Least confidence - Margin sampling - Ratio of confidence - Entropy	Query points where model is least confident	- Simple to implement - Computationally fast	- Can lead to unrepresentative queries - Sensitive to model uncertainty calibration	No
Query-by-Committee	- Maximum disagreement - Vote entropy - KL divergence	Use committee of models, query points of maximal disagreement	- Captures model uncertainty well	- Training multiple models is computationally expensive	Yes
Expected Model Change	Expected gradient length	Query points that impact maximal change to model parameters	- Directly maximizes information gain	- Computational cost of gradient calculations	Yes
Expected Error Reduction	Expected decrease in model error	Query points that maximize expected decrease in model error	- Directly reduces expected model error	- Requires accurate error estimation	Yes
Density-Weighted Methods	Informativeness and density	Combine informativeness with density for representative queries	- Improves query diversity	- Density estimation can be difficult in high dimensions	Depends on informativeness measure

Figure 2.12 – Comparison chart for query strategies

Figure 2.12 summarizes and compares various query strategies that have been discussed in this chapter.

Summary

In this chapter, we covered key techniques such as uncertainty sampling, query-by-committee, EMC, EER, and density weighting for designing effective active ML query strategies. Moving forward, in the next chapter, our focus will shift toward exploring strategies for managing the human in the loop. It is essential to optimize the interactions with the oracle labeler to ensure maximum efficiency in the active ML process. By understanding the intricacies of human interaction and leveraging this knowledge to streamline the labeling process, we can significantly enhance the efficiency and effectiveness of active ML algorithms.In the next chapter we will discuss how to manage the role of human labelers in active ML.

3

Managing the Human in the Loop

Active ML promises more efficient ML by intelligently selecting the most informative samples for labeling by human oracles. However, the success of these human-in-the-loop systems depends on effective interface design and workflow management. In this chapter, we will cover best practices for optimizing the human role in active ML. First, we will explore interactive system design, discussing how to create labeling interfaces that enable efficient and accurate annotations. Next, we will provide an extensive overview of the leading human-in-the-loop frameworks for managing the labeling pipeline. We will then turn to handling model-label disagreements through adjudication and quality control. After that, we will discuss strategies for recruiting qualified labelers and managing them effectively. Finally, we will examine techniques for evaluating and ensuring high-quality annotations and properly balanced datasets. By the end of this chapter, you will have the skills to build optimized human-in-the-loop systems that fully leverage the symbiosis between humans and AI.

In this chapter, we will discuss the following topics:

- Designing interactive learning systems and workflows
- Handling model-label disagreements
- Effectively managing human-in-the-loop systems
- Ensuring annotation quality and dataset balance

Technical requirements

In this chapter, we will be using the huggingface package, so you'll need to install it, as follows:

```
pip install datasets transformers huggingface_hub && apt-get install
git-lfs
```

Plus, you will need the following imports:

```
from transformers import pipeline
import torch
from datasets import load_dataset
import numpy as np
import pandas as pd
from sklearn.metrics import accuracy_score
```

Designing interactive learning systems and workflows

The effectiveness of a human-in-the-loop system depends heavily on how well the labeling interface and workflow are designed. Even with advanced active ML algorithms selecting the most useful data points, poor interface design can cripple the labeling process. Without intuitive controls, informative queries, and efficient workflows adapted to humans, annotation quality and speed will suffer.

In this section, we will cover best practices for optimizing the human experience when interacting with active ML systems. Following these guidelines will enable you to create intuitive labeling pipelines, minimize ambiguity, and streamline the labeling process as much as possible. We will also discuss strategies for integrating active ML queries, collecting labeler feedback, and combining expert and crowd labelers. By focusing on human-centered design, you can develop interactive systems that maximize the utility of human input for your models.

To begin, we'll provide definitions for the terms mentioned previously as they will be the main focus of this section.

A **labeling interface** is a user interface through which human annotators provide labels for data samples, such as *Roboflow*, *Encord*, and *LabelBox*, to name a few. It includes the visual presentation of each sample, as well as the controls and mechanisms for entering or selecting the desired labels. For example, an object detection labeling interface may display an image and provide tools to draw bounding boxes around objects and select class labels for each box. The annotator can then label cars, pedestrians, animals, and other objects appearing in the image using the interface controls. This can be seen in *Figure 3.1*, where the bounding boxes have been drawn around the dogs using the *dog* class:

Figure 3.1 – Example of a labeling interface where the annotator
is drawing bounding boxes around the dogs

Now, let's talk about workflows.

A **workflow** is the end-to-end sequence of steps that's followed by the annotator to complete the labeling task. It encompasses the full life cycle of a labeling job, from receiving the samples to be labeled, interacting with the interface to apply labels, submitting the completed annotations, and potentially handling exceptions or errors, as depicted in *Figure 3.2*. Optimizing the workflow involves streamlining these steps so that annotators can complete labeling efficiently. For an image classification task, the workflow may proceed as follows:

1. The annotator logs in to the labeling system and receives a batch of images to label.
2. The annotator is shown the first image and uses the interface to apply labels.
3. The annotator submits the labeled image and moves on to the next image.
4. After labeling the batch, the annotator submits the job, which triggers a reviewing stage for a quality check to be performed.
5. A reviewer checks the labeled images for accuracy and consistency.
6. If any errors are found, the images with incorrect annotations are returned to the annotator, at which point they need to re-label those images.
7. Once all the images pass the quality checks, the job is marked as complete:

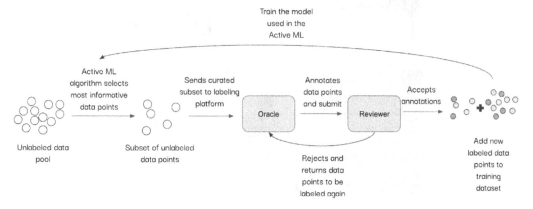

Figure 3.2 – Illustration of the labeling workflow

In short, the labeling interface focuses on the specific moment of interacting with an individual sample and applying labels. The workflow looks more holistically at the overall process and how to smoothly guide annotators through their labeling work. An effective human-in-the-loop system needs to design both aspects carefully around the human user.

Now that we know what a labeling interface and a workflow are, we understand that they can greatly impact the efficiency, accuracy, and overall quality of annotations in an active ML system. When designing interactive systems, there are several key considerations:

- **Intuitive and efficient interfaces**: The labeling interface should be intuitive and easy to use. When choosing the labeling interface that you want to use for a project, keep in mind that the UI the labelers will use has to be simple and efficient. For example, is it easy to draw a bounding box or a polygon around the objects of interest in a computer vision annotation project? Are there features to speed up the labeling process, such as using a pre-trained model such as Meta's **Segment Anything Model** (**SAM**) (https://segment-anything.com/), which can segment any object in images and pre-label the objects on the image? A good example of this is the Smart Polygon feature provided by the labeling platform Roboflow, which allows users to automatically label objects with polygons or bounding boxes, as shown in *Figure 3.3*. We will discuss Roboflow later in this chapter:

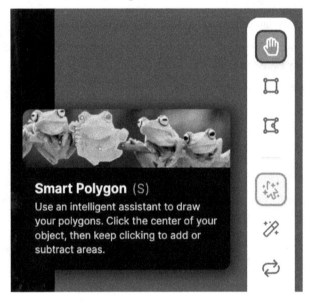

Figure 3.3 - Roboflow's Smart Polygon feature using SAM to automatically label objects on images, as demonstrated at https://blog.roboflow.com/automated-polygon-labeling-computer-vision/

- **Onboarding resources**: Minimal training should be required for labelers to use the labeling platform. To minimize the amount of training needed, an effective approach is to provide an onboarding document initially written by someone knowledgeable about using the labeling interface. This document can then be edited and updated by the labelers themselves as they learn how to overcome obstacles. This way, the training for labelers becomes less exhaustive as they can utilize the knowledge gained by each labeler and pass on what they've learned to new members joining the team.

- **Ontologies – naming convention**: An important consideration when designing a workflow for an annotation project is to carefully choose the names of the classes used for annotation. Having multiple spellings or words for the same class is a common issue. For example, in a project that aims to classify different types of pets, if a labeler decides to use the breed of the dog (for example, Australian Shepherd) instead of the class *dog*, it can cause issues later on. Fixing these issues is not always easy and can be time-consuming and expensive. Therefore, it is essential to select a labeling platform that allows the use of a labeling ontology. A **labeling ontology** is a structured vocabulary that provides a common understanding of how to label data, defines the classes, and outlines the relationships between different classes, especially in cases where nested structures exist. The ontology should also support the correction of typos or incorrect naming. In such cases, the names of the classes should be modifiable and update all objects labeled using that class. Additionally, the ontologies should be shareable across annotation projects to ensure consistency throughout. The ontology should support annotations of different styles, such as bounding boxes, polygons, classifications, and more. For example, the labeling platform Encord has a flexible labeling ontology feature, as depicted in *Figure 3.4*. We will discuss Encord later in this chapter:

Figure 3.4 – Encord's labeling ontology

- **Informative queries**: The samples that are presented to labelers should provide sufficient context and information to ensure clarity in the labeling task. This may involve providing complete documents or images instead of just extracts. Queries should be designed to minimize any potential ambiguity. For example, when using active ML to select the most informative frames for labeling from unlabeled videos, it is crucial to carefully organize the workflow to ensure that labelers are aware of the specific video they are labeling. In this case, the solution would be to ensure that the selected frames are separated by video and sorted before being sent to the labeling platform. The frames should then be presented to the labelers as a video with *jumps* due to the absence of non-selected frames. However, it is important to note that these missing frames do not remove the overall context entirely. The labeling platform Encord offers a solution for cases like this one with their feature called *image sequences*. Their image sequences format presents groups of images as a video to the labelers.

- **Automated workflows**: Labeling tasks should be automated as much as possible. The process of creating a task should involve minimal human intervention. One effective method for achieving this automation is by implementing a script that can run model inference on the unlabeled data pool, then use these predictions in the active ML sampling, particularly when utilizing uncertainty sampling, and, finally, send the selected data samples to the labeling platform and assign them to labelers and reviewers based on their availability.

- **Labeler feedback**: Allowing labelers to provide feedback or ask questions on difficult or ambiguous samples enables the annotation quality to improve over time. Therefore, the labeling platform should include a commenting and chatting system, which would allow labelers to help each other or seek guidance from field experts and reviewers.

By focusing on these aspects, you can create labeling systems that are adapted to human strengths and limitations. Well-designed interfaces and workflows result in more accurate, consistent, and efficient annotations, which are essential for the success of an ML project. Now, let's explore the current labeling platforms that you can consider.

Exploring human-in-the-loop labeling tools

Human-in-the-loop labeling frameworks are critical for enabling effective collaboration between humans and ML systems. In this section, we will explore some of the leading human-in-the-loop labeling tools for active ML.

We will look at how these frameworks allow humans to provide annotations, verify predictions, adjust model confidence thresholds, and guide model training through interfaces and workflows optimized for human-AI collaboration. Key capabilities provided by human-in-the-loop frameworks include annotation-assisted active ML, human verification of predictions, confidence calibration, and model interpretability.

The labeling tools we will examine include Snorkel AI, Prodigy, Encord, Roboflow, and others. We will walk through examples of how these tools can be leveraged to build applied active learning systems with effective human guidance. The strengths and weaknesses of different approaches will be discussed. By the end of this section, you will have a solid understanding of how to determine the right human-in-the-loop framework for your ML project based on your use case needs and constraints.

Common labeling platforms

Many labeling platforms offer a range of features for data labeling, including AI-assisted labeling, active ML, collaboration tools, and quality control tools. However, they vary in terms of pricing, model training, deployment capabilities, data management and curation tools, and model explainability features. For instance, when we examine six of the most frequently used labeling platforms, as depicted in *Figure 3.5*, we can observe these distinctions:

Feature	Snorkel AI	Encord	Roboflow	Prodigy	LabelBox	Dataloop
Data labeling	Yes	Yes	Yes	Yes	Yes	Yes
Model training	Yes	Yes	Yes	Yes	Yes	Yes
Model deployment	Yes	Yes	Yes	Yes	No	Yes
AI-assisted labeling	Yes	Yes	Yes	Yes	Yes	Yes
Integrated Active learning	Yes	Yes	Yes	Yes	Yes	Yes
Collaboration tools	Yes	Yes	Yes	Yes	Yes	Yes
Quality control tools	Yes	Yes	Yes	Yes	Yes	Yes
Data formats supported	Images, videos, text, audio	Images, videos, audio, DICOM	Images, videos	Text, Images, videos, audio	Images, videos, text, audio	Images, videos, LiDAR, audio, text

Figure 3.5 – Comparison table of six of the most common labeling platforms

Overall, all of the labeling platforms mentioned previously offer a variety of advantages and disadvantages. It is important to choose a platform that is well suited to the specific needs and requirements of the ML projects.

If you are seeking a platform with a wide array of features, including AI-assisted labeling, active learning, collaboration tools, and quality control, then Snorkel AI (https://snorkel.ai/), Encord (https://encord.com/), LabelBox (https://labelbox.com/), and Dataloop (https://dataloop.ai/) may be suitable options for you. On the other hand, if you require a platform specifically designed for **natural language processing** (**NLP**) tasks, then Prodigy (https://prodi.gy/) might be a good choice.

Next, we'll examine how to handle situations where the model and the human disagree.

Handling model-label disagreements

Disagreements between model predictions and human labels are inevitable. In this section, we will study how to identify and resolve conflicts.

Programmatically identifying mismatches

To identify discrepancies between the model's predictions and the human-annotated labels, we can write some simple Python code that highlights the mismatches for review.

Let's consider the example of an NLP sentiment classifier. This type of classifier is designed to analyze and understand the sentiment or emotions expressed in text. By examining the words, phrases, and context used in a given piece of text, an NLP sentiment classifier can determine whether the sentiment is positive, negative, or neutral. First, we will use the sentiment-analysis model from Huggingface:

```
sentiment_pipeline = pipeline("sentiment-analysis")
data = ["I love you", "I hate you"]
sentiment_pipeline(data)
```

The returns the following output:

```
[{'label': 'POSITIVE', 'score': 0.9998656511306763},
 {'label': 'NEGATIVE', 'score': 0.9991129040718079}]
```

The model correctly classifies these two sentences. Now, we want to study what flags a mismatch between a labeled dataset and the model's predictions for further review. So, we will download a labeled dataset from huggingface called *imdb*. This dataset is a large movie review dataset that's used for binary sentiment classification. We can load this dataset with the following line of code:

```
imdb = load_dataset("imdb")
```

For testing purposes, we'll only use a few samples:

```
small_dataset = imdb["train"].shuffle(seed=120).
    select([i for i in list(range(5))])
print(small_dataset)
```

This returns the following output:

```
Dataset({
    features: ['text', 'label'],
    num_rows: 5
})
```

We can take a better look at this dataset by looking at the last item in the dataset:

```
small_dataset[-1]
```

This gives us the following output:

```
{'text': "Shot into car from through the windscreen, someone is
playing someone else their latest song, someone else didn't react,
according to the voice-over. I just wonder how that came to be made.
There were too many scenes in this movie that I wondered about
how come a camera was there. If the scenes shot where the Warhols
descended on a BJM post-party are true then that was inexcusable
exploitation to the max, if not, then it was a total fabrication,
either way it made me uncomfortable, if that was the purpose? All the
way thru this movie I kept wondering how the footage came about. Taken
at face value, a nice portrait of the (tortured) genius we all believe
ourselves to be.",
'label': 1}
```

Here, we have a field called `text`, which provides a review of the movie, and a field called `label`, which classifies whether the sentiment is positive or negative. In this case, it is positive.

Let's gather the model's predictions on these five samples:

```
classes = ['NEGATIVE', 'POSITIVE']
results = []
for review in small_dataset['text']:
results.append(classes.index(sentiment_pipeline(review)[0]['label']))
print(results)
```

This returns the following output:

```
[1, 0, 0, 1, 0]
```

Now, to find out if we have mismatches with the original annotations from the dataset, we must define `x_true` and `y_true`, as follows:

```
y_true = np.array(small_dataset['label'])
x_true = np.array(small_dataset['text'])
```

Here, `x_true` is an array of the reviews and `y_true` is an array of labels. We can compare these to the model's predictions:

```
# Compare to true labels
mismatches = np.where(results != y_true)[0]

# Return mismatched samples
X_mismatched = x_true[mismatches]
```

```
y_mismatched = y_true[mismatches]

print(f"There are {len(X_mismatched)} mismatches: {X_mismatched}")
```

This returns the following output:

```
There are 2 mismatches: ['"Meatball Machine" has got to be one of the
most complex ridiculous, awful and over-exaggerated sci-fi horror
films that I have ever came across. It is about good against evil and
a coming-of-age tale, with the aim of to entertain with bloody, sleazy
and humorous context. Because of that the violence isn\'t particularly
gruesome and it doesn\'t make you squirm, but the gratuitous
bloodletting and nudity does run freely. The performances by Issei
Takahashi and Toru Tezuka is the worst i have seen, if that was not
enough it is also directed by an unheard of director called Yudai
Yamaguchi. This movie just have it all, it is bad to the bone!, A must
see for every b-movie freak!!!... Simply: an enjoying and rare gem.'
"Shot into car from through the windscreen, someone is playing someone
else their latest song, someone else didn't react, according to the
voice-over. I just wonder how that came to be made. There were too
many scenes in this movie that I wondered about how come a camera
was there. If the scenes shot where the Warhols descended on a BJM
post-party are true then that was inexcusable exploitation to the
max, if not, then it was a total fabrication, either way it made me
uncomfortable, if that was the purpose? All the way thru this movie I
kept wondering how the footage came about. Taken at face value, a nice
portrait of the (tortured) genius we all believe ourselves to be."]
```

Here, data points where the model and human disagree have been returned. These would be selected for additional review in this case.

Manual review of conflicts

After sampling the mismatched cases, we can do a manual review. Here are some example scenarios:

- The model predicts *dog* but the human labeled it as *cat*. On review, the photo quality was poor and it was a dog. This is a human error.

- The model predicts *negative* sentiment but the text was confidently *positive* according to the reviewer. This indicates a weakness in the model and needs to be fixed.

A manual review of model predictions provides valuable insights into the errors made by both the model and human labelers. One key strength is its ability to identify **systematic biases** in the training data, as well as cases where the model fails in ways that humans would not. However, a manual review is time-consuming and limited by human subjectivity and oversight. Typically, only a small subset of cases is reviewed, which may not uncover all weaknesses in the model. While a manual review serves as a useful debugging tool during model development, conducting large-scale reviews is often impractical. In such cases, alternative techniques such as active learning cycles may be necessary to further improve the model's robustness.

Another way to utilize mismatched sampling is by including the mismatched samples in the active ML pool for re-labeling. This allows for a better understanding of confusing cases and enables the model to be trained to handle such cases more effectively. This iterative process of continuously adding and re-labeling data helps fine-tune the model without the need for manual reviewing.

By systematically identifying, understanding, and resolving model-label disagreements, the system improves over time. The key is to maintain human oversight in the process. In the next section, we will talk about how to manage human-in-the-loop systems.

Effectively managing human-in-the-loop systems

Getting high-quality annotations requires finding, vetting, supporting, and retaining effective labelers. It is crucial to build an appropriate labeling team that meets the requirements of the ML project.

The first option is to establish an internal labeling team. This involves hiring full-time employees to label data, which enables close management and training. Cultivating domain expertise is easier when done internally. However, there are drawbacks to this, such as higher costs and turnover. This option is only suitable for large, ongoing labeling requirements.

Another option is to crowdsource labeling tasks using platforms such as ScaleAI, which allow labeling tasks to be distributed to a large, on-demand workforce. This option provides flexibility and lower costs, but it can lack domain expertise. Quality control becomes challenging when working with anonymous crowd workers.

You could use third-party labeling services, such as Innovatiana, which specializes in providing trained annotators for ML projects. This option leverages existing labeling teams and workflows. However, it can be more costly than crowdsourcing and challenging to manage.

Lastly, hybrid options are also doable. For example, you could use a mixed strategy that combines third-party labelers with internal reviewers. The optimal approach depends on budget, timelines, data sensitivity, field expertise, and project scope. A combination of sources provides flexibility. The key is instituting strong training, validation, and monitoring to get the quality needed from any labeling resource.

The next question here is how to manage the labeling team efficiently.

Managing a labeling team for maximum efficiency requires setting clear guidelines so that labelers understand expectations and the big-picture goals. As mentioned earlier in this chapter, workflows should be structured to optimize labelers' time, automating where possible and minimizing redundant tasks. Providing good tools is also key.

When feasible, give labelers access to dashboards and metrics so that they can see the growing dataset. This keeps them engaged in the process. For example, in *Figure 3.6*, we can see that in the Encord platform, the labelers can see how much they have labeled and how much they have left:

Instance label tasks status

An overview of the status of your instance labels

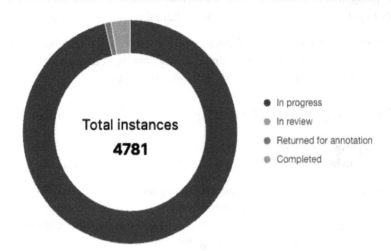

Total instances
4781

- In progress
- In review
- Returned for annotation
- Completed

Figure 3.6 – Encord's Instance label tasks status for an annotation project

Open communication channels allow labelers to easily discuss ambiguities, ask questions, and provide feedback. Make yourself accessible as a resource. Review labeling speed, accuracy, and costs to identify opportunities to improve productivity through enhancements to tools, training, or workflows.

Effective management also requires holding regular meetings to discuss progress, issues, and feedback. Designate senior labelers to help train and support newer members. Break large projects into stages with milestones to maintain focus. Highlight top performers and celebrate wins to motivate the team. Address underperformance through coaching and training.

With strong training, optimized workflows, communication, and performance management, a labeling team can work efficiently.

Another issue to be aware of and to address is that annotators can introduce biases based on their personal experiences, cultural backgrounds, or misunderstandings of the task at hand. This can lead to biased datasets where certain perspectives or characteristics are overrepresented or underrepresented, thus affecting the fairness and accuracy of ML models trained on these datasets. Biased annotations can potentially lead to AI models that perpetuate or even amplify these biases. This is particularly concerning in sensitive applications such as facial recognition, sentiment analysis, and predictive policing, where biased data can lead to unfair or discriminatory outcomes. As ML evolves, there's a growing emphasis on developing general-purpose foundational models that significantly reduce the reliance on extensive human labeling.

> **Note**
>
> A general-purpose foundational model is a versatile AI system that's been trained on vast amounts of data that can be adapted or fine-tuned to perform a wide range of tasks across different domains without the need for task-specific training from scratch.

An example of such innovation is SAM when it is used as a feature on labeling platforms to help accelerate labeling, which embodies the capability to understand and segment various objects in images or videos without the need for explicit, detailed human annotation for every new object type. This not only streamlines the development process by requiring less manual labeling but also aims to mitigate bias by relying on generalized learning capabilities that can adapt to diverse scenarios without inheriting the specific biases of a small group of human annotators. However, the design and training of these foundational models still necessitate careful consideration of the data they're trained on and the potential biases inherent in those datasets, highlighting the ongoing importance of fairness and ethical considerations in the field of AI.

Even with an efficient labeling team, can we ensure consistent quality of annotations over time? In the following section, we will explore this issue and discuss methods for ensuring the ongoing quality of annotations.

Ensuring annotation quality and dataset balance

Maintaining high annotation quality and target class balance requires diligent management. In this section, we'll look at some techniques that can help assure labeling quality.

Assess annotator skills

It is highly recommended that annotators undergo thorough training sessions and complete qualification tests before they can work independently. This ensures that they have a solid foundation of knowledge and understanding in their respective tasks. These performance metrics can be visualized in the labeling platform when the reviewers accept or reject annotations. If a labeler has many rejected annotations, it is necessary to ensure that they understand the task and assess what help can be provided to them.

It is advisable to periodically assess the labeler's skills by providing control samples for evaluation purposes. This ongoing evaluation helps maintain the quality and consistency of their work over time.

For example, designing datasets with known labels and asking the labelers to label these evaluation sets can be a good way to check if the task is well understood. Then, we can assess the accuracy of the annotations using a simple Python script.

First, we must define some dummy annotations that have been made by a labeler and some real annotations:

```
dummy_annotator_labels = ['positive', 'negative', 'positive',
    'positive', 'positive']
dummy_known_labels = ['negative', 'negative', 'positive', 'positive',
    'negative']
```

Then, we must calculate the accuracy and kappa score using the `sklearn` function:

```
accuracy = accuracy_score(dummy_annotator_labels, dummy_known_labels)
print(f"Annotator accuracy: {accuracy*100:.2f}%")
kappa = cohen_kappa_score(dummy_annotator_labels, dummy_known_labels)
print(f"Cohen's Kappa: {kappa:.3f}")
```

This returns the following output:

```
Annotator accuracy: 60.00%
Cohen's Kappa: 0.286
```

This technique is a simple and easy way to implement a basic assessment of the annotator's skills. Aim for an accuracy of above 90% and a kappa score of above 0.80 and then we can investigate poor agreements.

Use multiple annotators

If your budget allows, you can assign each data point to multiple annotators to identify conflicts. These conflicts can then be resolved through consensus or by an expert reviewer.

For example, with sentiment analytics labeling, we have our dummy annotations for three labelers:

```
dummy_annotator_labels_1 = ['positive', 'negative', 'positive',
    'positive', 'positive']
dummy_annotator_labels_2 = ['positive', 'negative', 'positive',
    'negative', 'positive']
dummy_annotator_labels_3 = ['negative', 'negative', 'positive',
    'positive', 'negative']
```

We can create a pandas DataFrame with the labels from the three labelers:

```
df = pd.DataFrame({
    "Annotator1": dummy_annotator_labels_1,
    "Annotator2": dummy_annotator_labels_2,
    "Annotator3": dummy_annotator_labels_3
})
```

Then, we can take the majority vote as a real label:

```
df["MajorityVote"] = df.mode(axis=1)[0]
print(df["MajorityVote"])
```

This returns the following output:

```
0    positive
1    negative
2    positive
3    positive
4    positive
```

This method can be expensive because the labelers work on the same data, but it can ultimately result in more accurate annotations. Its feasibility depends on the priorities of the ML project, as well as the budget and organization of the labeling team. For instance, if the labeling team consists of junior labelers who are new to the field, this method may be a suitable choice.

Balanced sampling

To prevent imbalanced datasets, we can actively sample minority classes at higher rates during data collection.

When collecting a dataset, it is important to monitor the distribution of labels across classes and adjust sampling rates accordingly. Without intervention, datasets often end up skewed toward majority classes due to their natural higher frequencies.

Let's look at some ways to actively sample minority classes at higher rates:

- Employing active ML approaches such as **uncertainty sampling** can bias selection toward rare cases. Indeed, uncertainty sampling actively selects the data points that the current model is least certain about for labeling. These tend to be edge cases and rare examples, rather than the common cases the model has already seen many examples of. Since, by definition, minority classes occur less frequently, the model is naturally more uncertain about these classes. So, uncertainty sampling will tend to pick more examples from the under-represented classes for labeling to improve the model's understanding.

- Checking label distributions periodically during data collection is important. If minority classes are underrepresented, it is recommended to selectively sample more data points with those labels. This can be achieved by sampling the data from the unlabeled data pool using a pre-trained model that can identify the unrepresented classes. To ensure higher representation, the sampling strategy should be set to select specific classes with a higher ratio. For example, let's reuse the *imdb* dataset from Hugging Face:

```
dataset = load_dataset('imdb')
```

For testing purposes, we assume that the dataset is unlabeled and that the labels attached to it are from the model's predictions. So, our goal is to sample the under-represented class. Let's assume class 0 is under-represented and we want to over-sample it. First, we must take the training dataset as our dummy unlabeled data pool and convert it into a pandas `DataFrame`:

```
dummy_unlabeled_dataset_with_predictions_from_a_model \
    dataset['train']
df = pd.DataFrame(
    dummy_unlabeled_dataset_with_predictions_from_a_model)
```

- Next, we must get the number of data points for each label:

```
n_label_0 = df[df['label'] == 0].shape[0]
n_label_1 = df[df['label'] == 1].shape[0]
```

- Now, we must calculate the number of samples to sample for each label, assuming we want to sample 1,000 samples and we want 80% of these samples to belong to class 0 and 20% to class 1:

```
nb_samples = 1000
n_sample_0 = int(0.8 * nb_samples)
n_sample_1 = int(0.2 * nb_samples)
sample_0 = df[df['label'] == 0].sample(n_sample_0,
    replace=False)
sample_1 = df[df['label'] == 1].sample(n_sample_1,
    replace=False)
# Concatenate the two samples into a single dataframe
sample_df = pd.concat([sample_0, sample_1], ignore_index=True)
# Print the sample dataframe
print(f"We have {len(sample_df['label'][sample_df['label']==0])}
class 0 samples and {len(sample_df['label'][sample_
df['label']==1])} class 1 samples")
```

This gives us the following output:

```
We have 800 class 0 samples and 200 class 1 samples
```

So, we sampled with the correct ratio and can, in theory, add these samples to our labeling queue next. By setting a higher sampling ratio for class 0 from the unlabeled data, we selectively oversample the minority class when getting new labeled data.

The key is closely tracking the evolving label distribution and steering sampling toward under-represented classes. This prevents highly imbalanced datasets that fail to provide sufficient examples for minority classes. The result is higher-quality, more balanced training data.

Summary

This chapter explored strategies for effectively incorporating human input into active ML systems. We discussed how to design workflows that enable efficient collaboration between humans and AI models. Leading open source frameworks for human-in-the-loop learning were reviewed, including their capabilities for annotation, verification, and active learning.

Handling model-label disagreements is a key challenge in human-AI systems. Techniques such as manually reviewing conflicts and active learning cycles help identify and resolve mismatches. Carefully managing the human annotation workforce is also critical as it covers recruiters, training, quality control, and tooling.

A major focus was ensuring high-quality balanced datasets while using methods such as qualification exams, inter-annotator metrics such as the accuracy or the Kappa score, consensus evaluations, and targeted sampling. By implementing robust processes around collaboration, conflict resolution, annotator management, and data labeling quality, the usefulness of human input in the loop can be maximized.

In the next chapter, we will shift our focus to applying active ML approaches specifically for computer vision tasks such as image classification, semantic segmentation, and object detection.

Part 2: Active Machine Learning in Practice

Building upon the foundational knowledge established in the first part, *Part 2* of this book transitions from theory to application, showcasing the powerful impact of active ML across various projects. This section is meticulously designed to demonstrate how active ML principles can be applied to solve real-world problems, emphasizing practical implementation with computer vision examples. Through detailed case studies and in-depth examples, readers will gain insight into the versatility and efficiency of active ML strategies when faced with the complexities of actual data.

This part includes the following chapters:

- *Chapter 4, Applying Active Learning to Computer Vision*
- *Chapter 5, Leveraging Active Learning for Big Data*

4

Applying Active Learning to Computer Vision

In this chapter, we will dive into using active learning techniques for computer vision tasks. Computer vision involves analyzing visual data such as images and videos to extract useful information. It relies heavily on machine learning models such as convolutional neural networks. However, these models require large labeled training sets, which can be expensive and time-consuming to obtain. Active ML provides a solution by interactively querying the user to label only the most informative examples. This chapter demonstrates how to implement uncertainty sampling for diverse computer vision tasks. By the end, you will have the tools to efficiently train computer vision models with optimized labeling effort. The active ML methods presented open up new possibilities for building robust vision systems with fewer data requirements.

By the end of this chapter, you will be able to do the following:

- Implementing active ML for an image classification project
- Applying active ML to an object detection project
- Using active ML for an instance segmentation project

Technical requirements

In this chapter, you will need to install the Ultralytics, PyYAML, and Roboflow packages.

Ultralytics is a popular open source Python library for building high-performance computer vision and deep learning models. It provides implementations of state-of-the-art object detection and image segmentation models including YOLO that can be trained on custom datasets.

PyYAML is a Python library used for reading and writing YAML files. YAML is a human-readable data serialization format. PyYAML allows loading YAML data from files or strings into Python data types such as dictionaries and lists. It can also dump Python objects back into YAML strings.

Roboflow, as presented in earlier chapters, is a platform that helps with preparing and managing datasets for computer vision models. It provides tools to annotate images, create training/test splits, and export labeled datasets in formats that are usable by deep learning frameworks such as PyTorch. Roboflow also integrates with libraries such as Ultralytics to streamline training pipelines. The main goal is to simplify the dataset management aspects of developing CV models.

To install these packages, we can run the following code:

```
pip install ultralytics && pip install pyyaml && pip install roboflow
```

You will also need the following imports:

```
import torch
from torch.utils.data import DataLoader, Subset
import torch.nn as nn
import torch.nn.functional as F
from torchvision import transforms
import torchvision
import torch.optim as optim
import matplotlib.pyplot as plt
import numpy as np
from tqdm import tqdm
from roboflow import Roboflow
import glob
import os
import yaml
import cv2
```

Additionally, you will need a Roboflow account in order to get a Roboflow API key. You can create an account here: https://app.roboflow.com/.

Implementing active ML for an image classification project

In this section, we will guide you through the implementation of active ML techniques for an image classification project. Image classification has various applications in computer vision, ranging from identifying products for an e-commerce website to detecting patterns of deforestation on geospatial tiles. However, creating accurate image classifiers requires extensive datasets of labeled images, which can be expensive and time-consuming to gather, as mentioned in *Chapter 1, Introducing Active Machine Learning*. Active ML offers a solution to this labeling bottleneck by interactively requesting the oracle to label only the most informative examples.

We will build an image classification model that will be capable of accurately classifying various images obtained from the CIFAR-10 dataset. This dataset is widely recognized in the field of computer vision and contains a diverse collection of 60,000 images, each belonging to one of 10 different classes. We will start with a small *labeled* set of only 2,000 images from CIFAR-10, then employ an active ML strategy to select the best images to present to an oracle for labeling. Specifically, we will use uncertainty sampling to query the examples the model is least certain about. We use uncertainty sampling here as it is simpler and less computationally expensive than other methods we have discussed previously. For instance, query-by-committee requires training multiple models, which is computationally expensive.

As more labels are acquired, model accuracy improves with fewer training examples. This demonstrates how active learning can create high-performing computer vision models with significantly lower data requirements.

Building a CNN for the CIFAR dataset

The implementation will cover initializing a **convolutional neural network (CNN)** classifier, training our model with a small labeled set, selecting unlabeled images for the next labeling step using active ML, acquiring new labels, retraining the model, and tracking model performance.

> **Quick reminder**
>
> A CNN classifier takes an image as input, extracts feature maps using convolutions, integrates the features in fully connected layers, and outputs predicted class probabilities based on what it learned during training. The convolutions allow it to automatically learn relevant visual patterns, making CNNs very effective for image classification tasks. You can find the PyTorch official tutorial on building a neural network model at `https://pytorch.org/tutorials/beginner/blitz/neural_networks_tutorial.html#sphx-glr-beginner-blitz-neural-networks-tutorial-py`.

Let's create a simple image classification model:

```
class Net(nn.Module):
    def __init__(self):
        super().__init__()
# First convolutional layer with 6 output channels, 5x5 kernel
        self.conv1 = nn.Conv2d(3, 6, 5)
# Max pooling layer with 2x2 window and default stride
        self.pool = nn.MaxPool2d(2, 2)
# Second convolutional layer with 16 output channels, 5x5 kernel
        self.conv2 = nn.Conv2d(6, 16, 5)

# First fully connected layer
# Flattened input size determined by conv2 output shape
```

```
        self.fc1 = nn.Linear(16 * 5 * 5, 120)

# Second fully connected layer with 84 nodes
        self.fc2 = nn.Linear(120, 84)

# Final fully connected output layer
# 10 nodes for 10 image classes
        self.fc3 = nn.Linear(84, 10)

    def forward(self, x):
# Pass input through first conv and activation
        x = self.pool(F.relu(self.conv1(x)))

# Second conv and activation, then pool
        x = self.pool(F.relu(self.conv2(x)))

# Flatten input for first fully connected layer
        x = torch.flatten(x, 1)

# Pass through all fully connected layers and activations
        x = F.relu(self.fc1(x))
        x = F.relu(self.fc2(x))
        x = self.fc3(x)

        return x
```

Note that we use this model because it is a small CNN that runs quickly and efficiently. This is helpful for running simple proofs of concept. However, next, we could use one of the pretrained models (such as **ResNet** at https://paperswithcode.com/method/resnet or **MobileNet** at https://paperswithcode.com/method/mobilenetv2) from torchvision, as follows:

```
from torchvision import models
model = models.resnet18(pretrained=True)
model = models.mobilenet_v2(pretrained=True)
```

You can find all the torchvision pretrained models on the library's model page: https://pytorch.org/vision/stable/models.html.

Now, we load the CIFAR-10 dataset with the appropriate transform function. The transform function defines a series of data processing and augmentation operations that are automatically applied when fetching samples from a PyTorch dataset. In the following code, we convert the images to tensors and normalize them:

```
transform = transforms.Compose(
[transforms.ToTensor(),
transforms.Normalize((0.5, 0.5, 0.5), (0.5, 0.5, 0.5))])

full_dataset = torchvision.datasets.CIFAR10(
    root='cifar10', train=True, download=True, transform=transform)
print(len(full_dataset))
```

This print shows us that the length of the full training dataset is 50,000 images. We are using the CIFAR-10 train dataset because we set the Boolean value of `train=True`. Later on, we will use the test set from CIFAR-10 and will then set `train=False`.

Now, we will create a small dataset of 2,000 labeled images. The purpose here is to simulate the existence of a small labeled set of images, while the remaining images are unlabeled. Our objective is to identify and select the most informative images for labeling next with active ML:

```
init_indices = list(range(2000)) # indices for initial our "labeled"
set
labeled_set = Subset(full_dataset, init_indices)
```

So, we have created a small labeled dataset and now need to initialize our training PyTorch data loader. A **PyTorch data loader** is used to load and iterate over datasets for training neural networks. It takes the dataset that contains the actual images and labels and is responsible for batching up these samples and feeding them to the model. The data loader allows you to specify a batch size, which determines how many samples are batched together – this is usually set to something like 64 or 128. Additionally, the data loader will shuffle the data by default if you are using it for a training set. This randomization of the order of samples helps the model generalize better during training:

```
# Data loaders
labeled_loader = DataLoader(labeled_set, batch_size=64, shuffle=True)
```

The next step is to initialize our model. We know that CIFAR-10 has 10 classes:

```
classes = ('plane', 'car', 'bird', 'cat', 'deer', 'dog', 'frog',
    'horse', 'ship', 'truck')
model = Net(n_classes=len(classes))
```

A good practice is to visualize the data with which we are working:

```
def imshow(img):
    img = img / 2 + 0.5      # unnormalize
    npimg = img.numpy()
    plt.imshow(np.transpose(npimg, (1, 2, 0)))
    plt.show()

# get some random training images
dataiter = iter(labeled_loader)
images, labels = next(dataiter)

# show images
imshow(torchvision.utils.make_grid(images))
```

Figure 4.1 depicts a sample of CIFAR-10 dataset images.

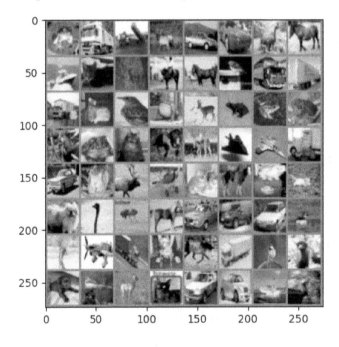

Figure 4.1 – A random visualization of some CIFAR-10 dataset images

It is also good to take a look at the labels, so let's print the first five labels:

```
print(' '.join(f'{classes[labels[j]]:5s}' for j in range(5)))
```

The preceding code returns the following list of labels as the output:

```
frog  truck truck deer  car
```

We can see that this is correct when cross-referencing these labels with the first five images in *Figure 4.1*.

What is unnormalizing?

Unnormalizing an image means reversing any normalization that was previously applied to the image pixel values in order to restore the original pixel value distribution (from the 0–1 range to the original 0–255 range).

Now that we have our data loader, we can start the training loop; we first define our loss and optimizer. The **loss function** measures how well the model's predictions match the true labels for a batch of images. It calculates the error between the predicted and true labels. Common loss functions for classification include cross-entropy loss and negative log-likelihood loss. These loss functions will output a high number if the model predicts incorrect labels, and a low number if the predictions are accurate. The goal during training is to minimize the loss by updating the model parameters. A good resource for learning about the loss functions available for use in PyTorch can be found here: `https://pytorch.org/docs/stable/nn.html#loss-functions`.

The **optimizer** is responsible for this parameter updating. It uses the loss value to perform backpropagation and update the model's weights and biases to reduce the loss. **Stochastic gradient descent (SGD)** is a popular optimization algorithm, where the parameters are updated proportionally to the gradient of the loss function. The learning rate controls the size of the updates. Other optimizers such as **Adam** and **RMSProp** are also commonly used for deep learning models (to learn about the optimizer functions available for use in PyTorch, you can visit this link: `https://pytorch.org/docs/stable/optim.html`):

```
criterion = nn.CrossEntropyLoss()
optimizer = optim.SGD(model.parameters(), lr=0.001, momentum=0.9)
```

We will train our model for 100 epochs. Epochs represent the number of passes through the full training dataset during the training of the model. We define a `train` function as follows to run our training:

```
def train(model, data_loader, epochs = 100):
    criterion = nn.CrossEntropyLoss()
    optimizer = optim.SGD(model.parameters(), lr=0.01, momentum=0.9)

    for epoch in range(epochs):  # loop over the dataset multiple
times
        running_loss = 0.0
        for i, data in enumerate(data_loader, 0):
# get the inputs; data is a list of [inputs, labels]
```

```
                inputs, labels = data

    # zero the parameter gradients
            optimizer.zero_grad()

    # forward + backward + optimize
            outputs = model(inputs)
            loss = criterion(outputs, labels)
            loss.backward()
            optimizer.step()

    # print statistics
            running_loss += loss.item()
            if i % 10 == 9:     # print every 10 mini-batches
                print(f'[{epoch + 1}, {i + 1:5d}] loss: {
                    running_loss / 2000:.3f}')
                running_loss = 0.0

    print('Finished Training')
    return model
```

Then, we run the training:

```
model = train(model, labeled_loader)
```

We have now an initial trained model on our small dataset and we want to use it to select the next images to label. But first, let's evaluate this model on the CIFAR-10 test set. We define an evaluation function:

```
def evaluate(model, test_dataset, batch_size=1):
    # Testing
    model.eval()
    test_loader = torch.utils.data.DataLoader(test_dataset,
        batch_size)

    correct = 0
    total = 0
    with torch.no_grad():
        for images, labels in tqdm(test_loader):
            outputs = model(images)
            _, predicted = torch.max(outputs.data, 1)
            total += labels.size(0)
            correct += (predicted == labels).sum().item()
```

```
print('\nAccuracy of the model on the test images: {}
    %'.format(100 * correct / total))
```

We can then use this function with our trained model once we define our test set as follows:

```
test_set = torchvision.datasets.CIFAR10(
    root='data', train=False, transform=transform, download=True)
print(len(test_set))
```

The test set's length is 10,000.

Let's use our evaluation function with this test set:

```
evaluate(model, test_set)
```

This gives us the following result:

```
Accuracy of the model on the test images: 40.08 %
```

So we have now tested our first trained model, which was trained on the 2,000 images of our initial small labeled set. The model's accuracy on the test set is 40.08%. We aim to improve this accuracy by labeling more images. This is where our active ML selection strategy comes into play.

Applying uncertainty sampling to improve classification performance

We will choose the most informative images to label next from our dataset – namely, the frames where the **model is least confident**, a method discussed in *Chapter 2, Designing Query Strategy Frameworks*.

We first define a function to get the model's uncertainty scores:

```
def least_confident_score(predicted_probs):
    return 1 - predicted_probs[np.argmax(predicted_probs)]
```

Then, we define our data loader for the unlabeled set. We will use a batch size of 1 as we will loop through all the images to get the uncertainty scores:

```
unlabeled_loader = DataLoader(full_dataset, batch_size=1)
```

We collect the confidence scores for our set of **unlabeled** images:

```
least_confident_scores = []
for image, label in unlabeled_loader:
    probs = F.softmax(model(image), dim=1)
    score = least_confident_score(probs.detach().numpy()[0])
    least_confident_scores.append(score)
print(least_confident_scores)
```

This returns the following:

```
[0.637821763753891, 0.4338147044181824, 0.18698161840438843,
0.6028554439544678, 0.35655343532562256, 0.3845849633216858,
0.4887065887451172, ...]
```

These values represent the **least confidence scores** of the model's predictions. The higher the scores, the less confident the model is. Therefore, next, we want to know the indices of the images where the scores are highest. We decide that we want to select 200 images (queries):

```
num_queries = 200
```

Then, we sort by uncertainty:

```
sorted_uncertainties, indices = torch.sort(
    torch.tensor(least_confident_scores))
```

We get the original indices of the most uncertain samples and print the results:

```
most_uncertain_indices = indices[-num_queries:]
print(f"sorted_uncertainties: {sorted_uncertainties} \
    nmost_uncertain_indices selected: {most_uncertain_indices}")
```

This returns the following:

```
sorted_uncertainties: tensor([0.0000, 0.0000, 0.0000,  ..., 0.7419,
0.7460, 0.7928], dtype=torch.float64)
most_uncertain_indices selected: tensor([45820, 36802, 15912,  8635,
32207, 11987, 39232,  6099, 18543, 29082, 42403, 21331,  5633, 29284,
29566, 23878, 47522, 17097, 15229, 11468, 18130, 45120, 25245, 19864,
45457, 20434, 34309, 10034, 45285, 25496, 40169, 31792, 22868, 35525,
31238, 24694, 48734, 18419, 45289, 16126, 31668, 45971, 26393, ...
44338, 19687, 18283, 23128, 20556, 26325])
```

Now we have the indices of the images selected using our active ML least-confident strategy. These are the images that would be sent to our oracles to be labeled and then used to train the model again.

Let's take a look at five of these selected images:

```
fig, axs = plt.subplots(1, 5)
for i in range(5):
    image, label = full_dataset[most_uncertain_indices[i]]
    image = image.squeeze().permute(1, 2, 0) / 2 + 0.5
    axs[i].imshow(image)
    axs[i].axis('off')
plt.show()
```

Figure 4.2 – Five of the chosen images to be labeled next

We have the images that now need to be labeled. Since this is a demo, we already have the labels, so let's retrain our model with these newly labeled images. First, we need to add those to our labeled set:

```
init_indices.extend(most_uncertain_indices)
labeled_set_2 = Subset(full_dataset, init_indices)
labeled_loader_2 = DataLoader(labeled_set, batch_size=64)
print(len(labeled_set_2))
```

This returns 2,200, which is correct because we first selected 2,000 images from our dataset and then queried 200 with our active ML sampling.

Let's start our training from scratch again for 100 epochs:

```
model_2 = Net(n_classes=len(classes))
model_2 = train(model_2, labeled_loader_2)
```

Then, run the evaluation on the test set:

```
evaluate(model_2, test_set)
```

This returns the following:

```
Accuracy of the model on the test images: 41.54 %
```

We have improved the accuracy on the test set from 40.08% to 41.54% by adding images selected with our active ML strategy to the training dataset. We could also fine-tune the model that was originally trained as follows:

```
model = train(model, labeled_loader_2)
evaluate(model, test_set)
```

This gives us the following:

```
Accuracy of the model on the test images: 40.84 %
```

We have an interesting result here: the fine-tuned model is performing worse than the model trained from scratch using the larger dataset. Overall, the model's performance improves when the selected images chosen by the active ML are added.

This approach can be applied to real-world problems. It is important to note, however, that this is a basic demonstration of how to use the least confident sampling method for classification. In a real project, you would need to have oracles label the selected images. Additionally, you would likely need to query more than 200 images and use a larger pretrained model, as mentioned earlier.

While the previous example demonstrated active ML for image classification, the same principles can be applied to other computer vision tasks such as object detection, as we'll see next.

Applying active ML to an object detection project

In this section, we will guide you through the implementation of active ML techniques for an object detection project. An object detection project refers to developing a computer vision model to detect and localize objects within images or videos. The dataset is a collection of images (video frames) containing examples of the objects you want to detect, among other things. The dataset needs to have labels in the form of bounding boxes around the objects. Popular datasets for this purpose include **COCO** (https://cocodataset.org/), **PASCAL VOC** (http://host.robots.ox.ac.uk/pascal/VOC/), and **OpenImages** (https://storage.googleapis.com/openimages/web/index.html). The model architecture uses a neural network designed for object detection such as Faster R-CNN, YOLO, and so on. This type of architecture can automatically identify and localize real-world objects within visual data. The end result is a model that can detect and draw boxes around objects such as cars, people, furniture, and so on.

The object detection project faces the same problem as classification projects: creating datasets is difficult and time-consuming. In fact, it is even more challenging for object detection tasks because it involves manually drawing bounding boxes around the objects. Once again, active ML provides a solution to this labeling bottleneck by sending the most informative images to the oracles for labeling. We will build an object detection model that will be capable of localizing brain tumors. This dataset we will use is from Roboflow Universe (https://universe.roboflow.com/) and is called *Brain Tumor Computer Vision Project*. To download this dataset, we use the Roboflow API:

```
rf = Roboflow(api_key="your_key")
project = rf.workspace("roboflow-100").project("brain-tumor-m2pbp")
dataset = project.version(2).download("yolov8")
```

This downloads the dataset locally. The dataset is downloaded as a folder with the structure shown in *Figure 4.3*.

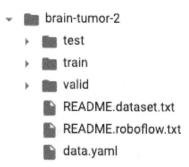

Figure 4.3 – Folder structure of the Roboflow Universe dataset, brain-tumor-m2pbp

Preparing and training our model

Next, we need to fix the data.yaml file to work properly in Google Colab and organize the data for our active ML demo. The data.yaml file is used in the ultralytics training to specify where the different sets (train, valid, and test) are placed. We assume here that the original training set is our unlabeled set of images, the validation set is our testing data, and the test set is our labeled data because it has the fewest examples. So, first, we define a function to rename the folders accordingly:

```
def rename_folders(current_folder_name, new_folder_name):
    # Check if the folder exists
    if os.path.exists(current_folder_name):
        # Rename the folder
        os.rename(current_folder_name, new_folder_name)
    else:
        print(f'The folder {current_folder_name} does not exist.')
# Now let's run it on our three folders train, valid, and test:

rename_folders(current_folder_name='/content/brain-tumor-2/train',
    new_folder_name='/content/brain-tumor-2/unlabeled')
rename_folders(current_folder_name='/content/brain-tumor-2/valid',
    new_folder_name='/content/brain-tumor-2/testing')
rename_folders(current_folder_name='/content/brain-tumor-2/test',
    new_folder_name='/content/brain-tumor-2/labeled')
```

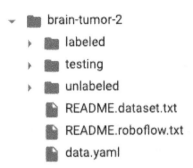

Figure 4.4 – Structure of the dataset after renaming the subfolders for our demo

Figure 4.4 shows the structure that we now have in our brain tumor dataset after renaming the folders for our demo. We then modify the data.yaml file:

```
path_data_yaml = '/content/brain-tumor-2/data.yaml'
with open(path_data_yaml, 'r') as file:
    data = yaml.safe_load(file)
data['train'] = 'labeled/images'
data['val'] = ''
data['test'] = 'testing/images'
with open(path_data_yaml, 'w') as file:
    yaml.dump(data, file)
```

Here, we renamed the subfolder paths in the data.yaml file, which is the file that we will use for our training. We do not want to use the val folder for now in our training.

Now let's take a look at our subfolders to determine the number of images in one of them:

```
unlabeled_files = glob.glob('/content/brain-tumor-2/unlabeled/
images/*.jpg')
labeled_files = glob.glob('/content/brain-tumor-2/labeled/images/*.
jpg')
testing_files = glob.glob('/content/brain-tumor-2/testing/images/*.
jpg')

print(f"For our demo, we have {len(unlabeled_files)} unlabeled files,
    {len(labeled_files)} labeled files, and {len(testing_files)}
    testing files")
```

The preceding code returns the following:

```
For our demo, we have 6930 unlabeled files, 990 labeled files, and
1980 testing files
```

We can now begin our initial training on our `labeled` dataset. For this training, we will utilize a widely used Python computer vision package called `ultralytics` (`https://github.com/ultralytics/ultralytics`) and employ the `yolov8` model. The `yolov8` model is capable of performing tasks such as detection and tracking, instance segmentation, image classification, and pose estimation. We will train our model for 10 epochs only for our demo purposes. We use the `detect` task type because we want to train the model for object detection:

```
from ultralytics import YOLO
model = YOLO('yolov8s.pt')
print('Start training ')
results = model.train(data=path_data_yaml,
    batch=32,
    task='detect',
    mode='train',
    epochs=10
    )
```

Analyzing the evaluation metrics

Once the training is done, we evaluate it on the test set. Here is how we can evaluate the model:

```
metrics = model.val(data=path_data_yaml, split='test')
print(metrics.results_dict)
```

The preceding returns the following output:

```
{'metrics/precision(B)': 0.6022637781613859,
 'metrics/recall(B)': 0.4763619681952341,
 'metrics/mAP50(B)': 0.4953616848732552,
 'metrics/mAP50-95(B)': 0.2252478418006819,
 'fitness': 0.25225922610793927}
```

Let's analyze these metrics:

- `precision(B)` measures how many of the predicted bounding boxes are correct. A value of 0.60 means 60% of the predicted boxes match the ground truth boxes.

- `recall(B)` measures how many of the ground truth boxes were correctly detected. A value of 0.48 means the model detected 48% of the true boxes.

- `mAP50(B)` is the mean average precision at the **intersection over union (IoU)** threshold of 50%, which measures the model's precision across different confidence thresholds. A prediction is considered correct if the IoU with ground truth is at least 50%. A value of 0.50 means the model has 50% mAP at this IoU threshold.

- mAP50-95 (B) is the mean average precision at IoU thresholds between 50% and 95% and is a more strict metric that expects higher overlap with the ground truth to be considered correct. The lower value of 0.23 indicates performance drops at higher IoU thresholds.

- fitness combines precision and recall. A model that scores high on precision but low on recall would have poor fitness. Similarly, high recall but low precision also results in low fitness. A high fitness score requires strong performance on both precision and recall metrics. This encourages the model to improve both the accuracy and completeness of detections during training. The specific fitness value of 0.25 here indicates there is significant room for improvement in precision, recall, or both.

The metrics indicate reasonably good precision but lower recall, meaning the model struggles to detect all ground truth boxes. The high precision but lower mAP shows many detections are offset from the ground truth. Overall, the metrics show room for improvement in the alignment and completeness of detections.

The next step is thus to select the most informative images to label using our active ML approach.

Implementing an active ML strategy

We will use the ultralytics package, which is highly useful for enabling the selection of informative images. This can help us improve the metrics we just discussed. This package provides the confidence score for each bounding box prediction, which we will utilize here.

We apply the model to each image in the unlabeled set using a confidence threshold of 0.15. This means that any predictions with a confidence score below 0.15 will be discarded. You can choose this value based on your specific needs and use case. It is important to keep in mind that choosing a low confidence score threshold allows for the selection of images where the model lacks confidence:

```
results = model(os.path.join('/content/brain-tumor-2/',
    'unlabeled/images'), verbose=False, conf=0.15)
```

Let's take a look at some of these images and the predicted bounding boxes:

```
plt.figure(figsize=(12, 8))
for i in range(1, 33):
    plt.subplot(4,8,i)
    image = results[i].orig_img
    for b in results[i].boxes.xywhn:
        x, y, w, h = b.tolist()
# Convert YOLO format coordinates to OpenCV format coordinates
        dh, dw, _ = image.shape
        l = int((x - w / 2) * dw)
        r = int((x + w / 2) * dw)
        t = int((y - h / 2) * dh)
```

```
        b = int((y + h / 2) * dh)
        cv2.rectangle(image, (l, t), (r, b), (0, 255, 0), 1)
    plt.imshow(image)
plt.show()
```

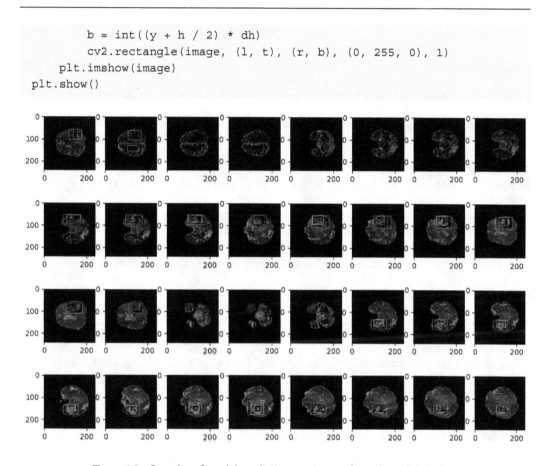

Figure 4.5 – Samples of model predictions on images from the unlabeled set

We can see in *Figure 4.5* that the model is detecting tumors in the unlabeled brain images.

Let's collect all the confidence scores of the predicted bounding boxes:

```
confidences = []
for result in results:
    confidences.append(result.boxes.conf)
```

We'll only keep the minimum confidence value for each image. If there is no predicted bounding box, we add a confidence score of 10 (a high value to put these images at the end of the list of potential images). Confidence scores are values ranging from 0 to 1, with 1 being high:

```
confidence_scores = []
for confidence in confidences:
    if len(confidence) > 0:
        confidence_scores.append(np.min(np.array(confidence.cpu())))
```

```
        else:
            confidence_scores.append(10)
    print(confidence_scores)
```

We have 6,930 confidence scores, which is correct because we have 6,930 unlabeled files.

Next, we select 500 images where the confidence scores are the lowest:

```
num_queries = 500
# Sort by uncertainty
sorted_uncertainties, indices = torch.sort(torch.tensor(confidence_
scores))
# Get original indices of most uncertain samples
most_uncertain_indices = indices[-num_queries:]
  print(f"sorted_uncertainties: {sorted_uncertainties[0:num_queries]} \
    nmost_uncertain_indices selected: {most_uncertain_indices}")
```

This returns the following:

```
sorted_uncertainties: tensor([0.1500, 0.1500, 0.1501, 0.1501, 0.1501,
0.1501, ..., 0.1598, 0.1598, 0.1598, 0.1599, 0.1599, 0.1599, 0.1599,
0.1599, 0.1600])
most_uncertain_indices selected: tensor([4714, 4713, 4712, 4304, 4305,
4306,  ...., 5554, 5553, 5552, 5551, 5550, 5549, 5548, 5547, 3135,
5544, 5543])
```

We now get the selected images with the following:

```
images_selected = np.array(
    glob.glob(os.path.join('/content/brain-tumor-2/',
        'unlabeled/images', '*.jpg'))
) [np.array(most_uncertain_indices)]
```

We move these selected images (and their corresponding label files) to our labeled set – this mimics the step where we would have an oracle label these images:

```
import shutil
for image_path in images_selected:
    shutil.move(image_path, image_path.replace('unlabeled',
        'labeled'))
    label_file = image_path.replace('images', 'labels').replace('.
jpg', '.txt')
    shutil.move(label_file, label_file.replace('unlabeled',
        'labeled'))
```

Let's check that we have correctly moved the images and label files:

```
images_labeled = glob.glob('/content/brain-tumor-2/labeled/images/*.
jpg')
labels_labeled = glob.glob('/content/brain-tumor-2/labeled/labels/*.
txt')
print(len(images_labeled))
print(len(labels_labeled))
```

These two `print` commands both return 1,490, which is what we expected because we had 990 labeled images and then added 500 new image/label pairs.

We can train our model again with this updated dataset:

```
model = YOLO('yolov8s.pt')
print('Start training ')
results = model.train(data=path_data_yaml,
     batch=32,
     task='detect',
     mode='train',
     epochs=10
     )
```

Then, we evaluate this model on the test set:

```
metrics = model.val(data=path_data_yaml, split='test')
metrics.results_dict
```

Now we get the following metrics:

```
{'metrics/precision(B)': 0.6469528069030884,
 'metrics/recall(B)': 0.5106541285546612,
 'metrics/mAP50(B)': 0.543579045283473,
 'metrics/mAP50-95(B)': 0.26662268193511757,
 'fitness': 0.29431831826995314}
```

Comparing these metrics with the previous metrics we got, we can see that the precision improved from 0.60 to 0.65, the recall from 0.48 to 0.51, the mAP50 from 0.50 to 0.54, the mAP50-95 from 0.22 to 0.27, and the fitness from 0.25 to 0.29. So, adding the 500 most informative images to our labeled set improved our metrics across the board.

We can use a similar method for instance segmentation, which we will cover in the next section.

Using active ML for a segmentation project

In this section, we will reuse what we did for the object detection task, but instead of using an object detection dataset, we will use an instance segmentation dataset with the segment task of yolov8.

Instance segmentation is a computer vision task that involves detecting and segmenting individual objects in an image at the pixel level. It combines elements of object detection, which localizes objects by drawing bounding boxes around them, and semantic segmentation, which classifies each pixel in the image according to the class it belongs to. Instance segmentation goes a step further – it assigns an instance label to each segmented object. The output is a set of masks, one per detected object instance, that indicate the exact pixels that belong to each object. Instance segmentation provides a more detailed delineation of objects compared to the bounding boxes produced in object detection. It segments objects at the pixel level rather than just enclosing them in boxes. It also goes beyond semantic segmentation, which only distinguishes between classes such as person, car, and so on. Instance segmentation separates individual instances of those classes – person 1 versus person 2, or car 1 versus car 2.

The combination of localization, classification, and separation of instances enables precise analysis of images down to the pixel level. This makes instance segmentation useful for applications such as autonomous driving, medical imaging, and robotics, where understanding scenes at a fine-grained level is required. Some popular instance segmentation algorithms and models are **Mask R-CNN** (https://arxiv.org/abs/1703.06870), **Panoptic FPN** (https://arxiv.org/abs/1901.02446), and **YOLACT** (https://arxiv.org/abs/1904.02689).

Let's download the strawberry dataset from Roboflow Universe

```
rf = Roboflow(api_key="your_key")
project = rf.workspace("5060tanapoowapat-yumsarn").
project("strawberry-2vs5u")
dataset = project.version(2).download("yolov8")
```

Then, we work through the same steps as we followed for the object detection dataset in the preceding section. We rename the subfolders for our demo use case and update the YAML file. We end up with the structure shown in *Figure 4.6*.

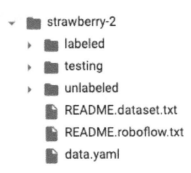

Figure 4.6 – Structure of the strawberry dataset after renaming the subfolders for our demo

For this dataset, after renaming the folders and updating the YAML file, the code returns the following:

```
For our demo, we have 3006 unlabeled files, 184 labeled files, and 659
testing files
```

As we are now training for instance segmentation, we update the training code as follows:

```
model = YOLO('yolov8n-seg.pt')
print('Start training ')
results = model.train(data=path_data_yaml,
    batch=16,
    task='segment',
    mode='train',
    epochs=10
    )
```

Once the training is completed, we evaluate the model using the same code as in the previous project and obtain the following metrics:

```
{'metrics/precision(B)': 0.673169825129636,
 'metrics/recall(B)': 0.7297833796885302,
 'metrics/mAP50(B)': 0.7664149988792639,
 'metrics/mAP50-95(B)': 0.533442993245899,
 'metrics/precision(M)': 0.7415224838967787,
 'metrics/recall(M)': 0.7482014388489209,
 'metrics/mAP50(M)': 0.8165979711704425,
 'metrics/mAP50-95(M)': 0.5967313838152124,
 'fitness': 1.175458236359971}
```

The metrics with (B) represent the metrics for object detection, while the metrics with (M) refer to instance segmentation, where M stands for masks. The metrics are the same between the two types; the only difference is that the M metrics are computed on the pixels from the masks rather than those from the bounding boxes.

Following the same logic, we then select the images to label in order to improve our metrics.

The code is slightly different this time when we run the model on each image in the unlabeled set:

```
results = model(os.path.join(f'/content/{dataset_name}/',
    'unlabeled/images'), verbose=False, conf=0.25, task='segment')
```

We have to specify that we are performing a segmentation task and choose a higher confidence threshold to avoid memory issues in Colab.

Let's take a look at the model's predictions on some of the unlabeled images:

```
plt.figure(figsize=(12, 8))
# Generate a list of 32 random integers between 0 and 100
random_integers = [random.randint(0, 100) for _ in range(32)]
for i, index in enumerate(random_integers):
    plt.subplot(4,8,i+1)
    image = results[index].orig_img
    for b in results[index].boxes.xywhn:
        x, y, w, h = b.tolist()
        # Convert YOLO format coordinates to OpenCV format coordinates
        dh, dw, _ = image.shape
        l = int((x - w / 2) * dw)
        r = int((x + w / 2) * dw)
        t = int((y - h / 2) * dh)
        b = int((y + h / 2) * dh)
    cv2.rectangle(image, (l, t), (r, b), (0, 255, 0), 2)

    if results[index].masks:
        overlayed_image = image.copy()
        for m in results[index].masks:
            # Make sure both images are of data type uint8
            mask = np.array(m.data.cpu()[0])
            mask = cv2.cvtColor(mask, cv2.COLOR_GRAY2BGR)
            image = image.astype(np.uint8)
            mask = mask*255
            mask = mask.astype(np.uint8)

            # Overlay the mask on the RGB image
            overlayed_image = cv2.addWeighted(overlayed_image, 1,
                mask, 0.8, 0)

    plt.imshow(cv2.cvtColor(overlayed_image, cv2.COLOR_BGR2RGB))
plt.show()
```

This returns the image depicted in *Figure 4.7*.

Figure 4.7 – Samples of model predictions on images from the unlabeled set

In *Figure 4.7*, we can see that the model is correctly detecting most of the strawberries. The object detection is represented by the green bounding boxes in the images, while the segmentation is indicated by the white overlaying masks.

We then follow the steps discussed in the preceding section on object detection, where we selected the 500 images to label next, and we get the following result:

```
sorted_uncertainties: tensor([0.2500, 0.2501, 0.2501, 0.2501, 0.2501,
0.2502, 0.2503, 0.2503, 0.2503, 0.2503, 0.2503,..., 0.2703, 0.2703,
0.2703, 0.2703, 0.2703, 0.2704, 0.2704, 0.2704, 0.2704, 0.2704])
most_uncertain_indices selected: tensor([2744,  806, 1822, 1025,
1486,  345,  743, 1374, 2329, 1381,  301, 2322, 2272, 1196, ..., 2127,
2004, 2119, 2118, 1401, 1402, 2666, 2105,  100,   47, 2093,   46,
2092, 2085,  970, 1422])
```

We move these images to our labeled set, and thus go from 184 images in the labeled set to 684. We run the training on the updated labeled set, followed by the evaluation, and obtain these metrics:

```
{'metrics/precision(B)': 0.7522007556106134,
'metrics/recall(B)': 0.7570614064930203,
'metrics/mAP50(B)': 0.800552933790843,
'metrics/mAP50-95(B)': 0.6079730626509038,
```

```
'metrics/precision(M)': 0.8061734224988162,
'metrics/recall(M)': 0.8069544364508393,
'metrics/mAP50(M)': 0.8511208111235853,
'metrics/mAP50-95(M)': 0.6554160034789296,
'fitness': 1.3022175340082929}
```

Let's compare those to the metrics we had before the addition of the 500 most informative images:

```
{'metrics/precision(B)': 0.673169825129636,
'metrics/recall(B)': 0.7297833796885302,
'metrics/mAP50(B)': 0.7664149988792639,
'metrics/mAP50-95(B)': 0.533442993245899,
'metrics/precision(M)': 0.7415224838967787,
'metrics/recall(M)': 0.7482014388489209,
'metrics/mAP50(M)': 0.8165979711704425,
'metrics/mAP50-95(M)': 0.5967313838152124,
'fitness': 1.175458236359971}
```

We can observe that all metrics have improved.

Summary

In conclusion, this chapter has demonstrated how active ML can be applied to optimize the training of computer vision models. As we have seen, computer vision tasks such as image classification, object detection, and instance segmentation require large labeled datasets to train **convolutional neural networks (CNNs)**. Manually collecting and labeling this much data is expensive and time-consuming.

Active ML provides a solution to this challenge by intelligently selecting the most informative examples to be labeled by a human oracle. Strategies such as uncertainty sampling query the model to find the data points it is least certain about. By labeling only these useful data points, we can train our models with significantly less data-labeling effort required.

In this chapter, we covered implementing active ML approach for diverse computer vision applications. By interactively querying the model and refining the training data, we can rapidly improve model performance at a fraction of the labeling cost. These techniques make it feasible to develop computer vision systems even with limited data.

The active ML implementations presented offer new possibilities for building performant and robust computer vision models without needing massive datasets. With these strategies, you can optimize and target the data collection and training efforts for efficient results. Going forward, active ML will become an essential tool for developing real-world computer vision systems.

In the next chapter, we will explore how to leverage active ML for big data projects that use large amounts of data, such as videos.

5

Leveraging Active Learning for Big Data

In this chapter, we will explore how to use **machine learning** (**ML**) to deal with big data, such as videos. The task of developing ML models for video analysis comes with its own set of unique challenges. Videos, being inherently large, pose significant hurdles in terms of efficient processing. Video analysis using ML has become an increasingly important technique across many industries and applications. From autonomous vehicles that rely on computer vision models to analyze road conditions in real-time video feeds, to security systems that can automatically detect suspicious activity, ML is revolutionizing what's possible with video data. These models can automate time-consuming manual analysis and provide scalable video understanding. Implementing performant and scalable video analysis pipelines involves surmounting key hurdles such as an enormous amount of data labeling.

We will guide you through a cutting-edge ML method that will aid you in selecting the most informative frames for labeling, thereby enhancing the overall accuracy and efficacy of the analysis.

In this chapter, we will cover the following topics:

- Implementing ML models for video analysis
- Selecting the most informative frames with Lightly

Technical requirements

In this chapter, you will need to install the following packages:

```
pip install ultralytics lightly docker encord
```

You will also need the following imports:

```
import os
from IPython.display import display, Markdown
from ultralytics import YOLO
```

```
from pathlib import Path
import json
import contextlib
from typing import Iterator
import docker
from docker.models.containers import Container
from lightly.api import ApiWorkflowClient
from lightly.openapi_generated.swagger_client import DatasetType
from lightly.openapi_generated.swagger_client import DatasourcePurpose
from encord.orm.cloud_integration import CloudIntegration
from encord.orm.dataset import AddPrivateDataResponse
from encord.user_client import EncordUserClient
from encord.orm.dataset import CreateDatasetResponse, StorageLocation
```

Next, you need to create a Lightly account and set up your API token, as follows:

```
lightly_token = "your_lightly_token"
```

Then, you must set up the Lightly client to connect to the API:

```
client = ApiWorkflowClient(token=lightly_token)
```

This demo was run on an AWS SageMaker notebook (`ml.g4dn.2xlarge instance`). This instance has a GPU and enough memory to run this demo because we need access to Docker, which is not possible in Google Colab.

An Encord account (`https://app.encord.com/`) is also required if you want to send the selected frames to an annotation platform.

Implementing ML models for video analysis

Active ML plays a transformative role in managing big data projects by strategically optimizing the data annotation process, thereby enhancing model performance with less manual effort. For instance, in large-scale image recognition tasks, such as identifying specific objects across millions of social media photos, active learning can significantly reduce the workload by pinpointing images that are most likely to refine the model's capabilities. Similarly, in **natural language processing** (**NLP**) applications, dealing with vast amounts of text data from sources such as news articles, forums, and customer feedback, active ML helps in selectively annotating documents that add the most value to understanding complex language nuances or sentiments. This approach not only streamlines the effort required in annotating massive datasets but also ensures that models trained on such data are more accurate, efficient, and capable of handling the real-world variability inherent in big data sources. Extending this methodology to video analysis, active ML becomes even more pivotal due to the added complexity and volume of data within video content. Active ML can be leveraged to identify key frames or segments that significantly contribute to the model's learning, dramatically reducing the annotation burden while ensuring comprehensive understanding and analysis of video data. This targeted approach in video projects not only conserves resources but also accelerates the development of sophisticated video analysis models that are capable of performing tasks such as activity recognition, event detection, and sentiment analysis with higher precision and efficiency.

In this section, we will explore how to leverage active ML for developing an ML model for videos. ML video analysis systems require implementing strategies to efficiently curate video frames. Videos are usually large files, and annotating all frames in the videos is impossible. Moreover, depending on the **frames per second** (**FPS**) rate, videos often contain a significant amount of duplicated data, which would be a waste of time and money to label. Common practice is to label at an FPS rate of 1, instead of 30 for example, to reduce the number of frames to label. However, this is not an optimal solution as it will lead to similar frames being annotated, an imbalance in the classes that are represented, and a lack of diversity in the data selected. Plus, many of the frames that will be labeled if such a pipeline is in place probably don't need to be labeled in the first place because the model might already perform very well on some of those frames. Thus, labeling frames on which the model is confident and correct is a waste of time and money.

In other words, it is infeasible to manually label all frames in video datasets for ML, making active learning crucial due to the following factors:

- **Data volume**: Video data consists of a large number of frames, which makes comprehensive manual labeling extremely time-consuming and expensive. For instance, labeling objects in all frames of just 10 minutes of a 30 FPS video would require labeling 18,000 images.

- **Redundancy**: Consecutive video frames are highly redundant as they contain almost identical content. It is inefficient to manually label this repetitive data.

- **Cost**: The expense of hiring human labelers to meticulously annotate video frames would be exorbitant, rendering the majority of projects economically unfeasible. Labeling fees for just 10 hours of video could amount to thousands of dollars.

This is where active ML is invaluable. It optimizes the labeling effort by identifying the most informative frames that are likely to improve the model, as we have seen in previous chapters. Human labelers can then focus exclusively on these high-value frames. By directing the labeling process to maximize performance gains, considerably fewer frames require manual annotation, making video ML viable and cost-effective.

In summary, exhaustive manual video data labeling is impractical and economically unfeasible. Active learning provides crucial optimization for labeling so that models can be trained to analyze video in a feasible, affordable, and adaptable manner.

Now, let's explore a real-world example with a commonly used active ML tool called **Lightly** (`https://www.lightly.ai/`).

Selecting the most informative frames with Lightly

In this section, we will use an active ML tool called **Lightly**. Lightly is a data curation tool that's equipped with a web platform that enables users to choose the optimal subset of samples for maximizing model accuracy. Lightly's algorithms can process substantial volumes of data, such as 10 million images or 10 thousand videos, in less than 24 hours.

The web app allows users to explore their datasets using filters such as sharpness, luminance, contrast, file size, and more. They can then use these filters to explore correlations between these characteristics.

Users can also search for similar images or objects within the app and look into the embeddings (**principal component analysis (PCA)**, **T-distributed stochastic neighbor embedding (TSNE)**, and **uniform manifold approximation and projection (UMAP)**). Embeddings refers to vector representations of images that are learned by deep neural networks. They capture visual features and semantics of the images in a way that allows similarities and relationships between images to be analyzed. When images are passed through a convolutional neural network, the final layer before classification is typically a dense representation of the image features. This dense layer outputs a vector with hundreds or thousands of dimensions for each image. This vector is called an embedding. Images with similar features will have embeddings that are close or nearby when mapped in the embedding space. Images with very different features will be farther apart in the embedding space.

There are a few techniques that can be used to visualize these high-dimensional embeddings in two or three dimensions for human analysis:

- **PCA**: PCA reduces the dimensions of embeddings down to 2D or 3D so that they can be plotted. It projects them onto the dimensions that capture the most variance. Images with similar prominent visual features will appear closer together after PCA projection.

- **TSNE**: TSNE is a technique that represents high-dimensional embeddings in lower dimensions while keeping similar images close and dissimilar images apart. The 2D or 3D mappings attempt to model the local structure of the higher dimensional space.

- **UMAP**: UMAP is a more recent technique that can preserve global data structure in the projections better than TSNE in many cases. It maps images with similar embeddings nearby and dissimilar ones farther apart in the projection.

Embeddings capture image features and semantics in vectors. Techniques such as PCA, TSNE, and UMAP then project these high-dimensional vectors down to 2D or 3D so that they can be visualized and analyzed for similarity relationships between images. The Lightly app leverages these projections to enable image similarity searches.

Using Lightly to select the best frames to label for object detection

To select the best frames, we need to conduct a series of steps.

Dataset and pre-trained model

In this example, we will use a video of a dog running after a ball. We will only be using one video, as depicted in *Figure 5.1*, for demo purposes. This video can be found in this book's GitHub repository (`https://github.com/PacktPublishing/Active-Machine-Learning-with-Python/blob/main/Chapter_5/videos/project_demo/dog_running_ball.mp4`):

Figure 5.1 – Video used for testing our Lightly demo

Our main goal in this section is to select the most informative frames in this video using the different sampling strategies that Lightly offers.

Our video called `dog_running_ball.mp4` is stored in a subfolder called `project_demo` under a folder called `videos`.

Once, we have the video in our `videos/project_demo` folder, the next step is to load a pre-trained object detection model:

```
Model = YOLO("yolov8x.pt")
```

This pre-trained model from `ultralytics` supports 80 classes that we can visualize with the following command:

```
model.namesg
```

This returns the following output:

```
{0: 'person',
 1: 'bicycle',
 2: 'car',
 3: 'motorcycle',
 ...
 32: 'sports ball',
 33: 'kite',
 34: 'baseball bat',
 ...
 76: 'scissors',
 77: 'teddy bear',
 78: 'hair drier',
 79: 'toothbrush'}
```

In our case, we know we are dealing with a video of a dog running after a ball, so we will focus on the dog and sports ball classes.

Then, we must prepare some of the variables for our Lightly run, such as the path to the predictions output folder, the task's name, and the important classes that we want to focus on in this run to improve our model (dog and sports ball):

```
important_classes = {"dog": 16, " sports ball": 32}
classes = list(important_classes.values())
```

Our classes here are 16 and 32.

Creating the required Lightly files

We will be saving our inference predictions in a subfolder called predictions; our task name is yolov8_demo_dog_detection:

```
predictions_rooth_path = Path("predictions")
task_name = "yolov8_demo_dog_detection"
predictions_path = Path(predictions_rooth_path / task_name)
```

Then, we need to create all the configuration files that Lightly will use:

- The tasks.json file, which specifies the name of our current task. A task name is the name of the corresponding subfolder in the folder predictions.

- The schema.json file, which allows Lightly to know the format of the predictions.

- The metadata schema.json file, which contains the names of the videos in our videos folder.

The code to create these configuration files can be found in the Chapter 5 section in this book's GitHub repository (https://github.com/PacktPublishing/Active-Machine-Learning-with-Python/tree/main/Chapter_5).

We can now run object detection inference using the pre-trained model we loaded earlier.

Inference

We'll run object detection inference on our test video with a low confidence threshold of 0.3 as we want to have lower confidence scores. The code has been set up to handle more than one video in the subfolder. However, for testing purposes, we only have one video. We will skip predictions that are not part of the important classes:

```
videos = Path("videos/project_demo/").glob("*.mp4")
for video in videos:
    print(video)
    results = model.predict(video, conf=0.3)
    predictions = [result.boxes.data for result in results]
    number_of_frames = len(predictions)
    padding = len(str(number_of_frames))
    fname = video
    for idx, prediction in enumerate(predictions):
        populate_predictions_json_files(prediction, fname, padding)
```

The populate_predictions_json_files function is defined in the code in this book's GitHub repository (https://github.com/PacktPublishing/Active-Machine-Learning-with-Python/tree/main/Chapter_5).

Once we have run this code, we'll receive the outputs of the inference run in the format supported by Lightly in the `predictions` subfolder, as shown in *Figure 5.2*:

```
!ls predictions/yolov8_demo_dog_detection
dog_running_ball-000-mp4.json    dog_running_ball-148-mp4.json
dog_running_ball-001-mp4.json    dog_running_ball-149-mp4.json
dog_running_ball-002-mp4.json    dog_running_ball-150-mp4.json
dog_running_ball-003-mp4.json    dog_running_ball-151-mp4.json
dog_running_ball-004-mp4.json    dog_running_ball-152-mp4.json
dog_running_ball-005-mp4.json    dog_running_ball-153-mp4.json
dog_running_ball-006-mp4.json    dog_running_ball-154-mp4.json
dog_running_ball-007-mp4.json    dog_running_ball-155-mp4.json
dog_running_ball-008-mp4.json    dog_running_ball-156-mp4.json
dog_running_ball-009-mp4.json    dog_running_ball-157-mp4.json
dog_running_ball-010-mp4.json    dog_running_ball-158-mp4.json
dog_running_ball-011-mp4.json    dog_running_ball-159-mp4.json
dog_running_ball-012-mp4.json    dog_running_ball-160-mp4.json
dog_running_ball-013-mp4.json    dog_running_ball-161-mp4.json
dog_running_ball-014-mp4.json    dog_running_ball-162-mp4.json
dog_running_ball-015-mp4.json    dog_running_ball-163-mp4.json
dog_running_ball-016-mp4.json    dog_running_ball-164-mp4.json
dog_running_ball-017-mp4.json    dog_running_ball-165-mp4.json
dog_running_ball-018-mp4.json    dog_running_ball-166-mp4.json
dog_running_ball-019-mp4.json    dog_running_ball-167-mp4.json
dog_running_ball-020-mp4.json    dog_running_ball-168-mp4.json
dog_running_ball-021-mp4.json    dog_running_ball-169-mp4.json
dog_running_ball-022-mp4.json    dog_running_ball-170-mp4.json
dog_running_ball-023-mp4.json    dog_running_ball-171-mp4.json
dog_running_ball-024-mp4.json    dog_running_ball-172-mp4.json
dog_running_ball-025-mp4.json    dog_running_ball-173-mp4.json
dog_running_ball-026-mp4.json    dog_running_ball-174-mp4.json
dog_running_ball-027-mp4.json    dog_running_ball-175-mp4.json
```

Figure 5.2 – Lightly JSON predictions (snapshot)

If we take a look at one of those files, the information the JSON files contain is the result of the inference. This includes the coordinates of the bounding boxes, along with the corresponding class ID and confidence score, as shown in *Figure 5.3*:

```
▼ root:
    file_name: "dog_running_ball-000-mp4.png"
  ▼ predictions: [] 2 items
    ▼ 0:
        category_id: 16
      ▼ bbox: [] 4 items
          0: 945
          1: 484
          2: 432
          3: 501
        score: 0.9555591344833374
    ▼ 1:
        category_id: 32
      ▼ bbox: [] 4 items
          0: 894
          1: 300
          2: 36
          3: 37
        score: 0.7985605597496033
```

Figure 5.3 – Prediction JSON file for the first frame in the format expected by Lightly

We are now ready to schedule the active Lightly ML run.

Schedule the active ML run

We can register the Lightly worker using the following code, which returns the ID of our Lightly worker:

> **Note**
> If a worker with this name already exists, the ID of the existing worker will be returned.

```
worker_id = client.register_compute_worker(name="Demo")
```

Lightly uses Docker to run active ML with the lightly/worker:latest image. It can be pulled using the command line:

```
docker pull lightly/worker:latest
```

Docker is an open platform for developing, shipping, and running applications within software containers. It allows code to be packaged with all its dependencies and libraries into a standardized unit for software development. Using Docker containers eliminates compatibility issues that arise from differences between environments. In short, it enables easy replicability when running scripts because the environment in the Docker image is already set up with the correct installed packages.

Next, we need to schedule our active ML run. This process involves several steps:

1. Create a Lightly dataset called `demo_dataset`:

    ```
    client.create_dataset(dataset_name="demo_dataset",
        dataset_type=DatasetType.VIDEOS)
    dataset_id = client.dataset_id
    ```

2. Set up the data sources by using the `project_demo` project as the input or output locations for data. In our case, we are using the local storage option (`https://docs.lightly.ai/docs/local-storage`) for demo purposes, but ideally, you should use the cloud service option (`https://docs.lightly.ai/docs/cloud-storage`), which uses either AWS, Azure, or GCP:

    ```
    client.set_local_config(
        relative_path="project_demo",
        purpose=DatasourcePurpose.INPUT
    )
    client.set_local_config(
        relative_path="project_demo",
        purpose=DatasourcePurpose.LIGHTLY
    )
    ```

3. Schedule the active ML run with the selected strategies we want to use: a strategy to find diverse objects, a strategy to balance the class ratios, and a strategy to use a prediction score for the object's frequencies and least confident results. We are sampling five samples in this example and are trying to reach a 50/50 balance between the `dog` and `sports ball` classes:

    ```
    scheduled_run_id = client.schedule_compute_worker_run(
        worker_config={},
        selection_config={
            "n_samples": 5,
            "strategies": [
                {
                    # strategy to find diverse objects
                    "input": {
                        "type": "EMBEDDINGS",
                        "task": task_name,
                    },
    ```

```
                "strategy": {
                    "type": "DIVERSITY",
                },
            },
            {
                # strategy to balance the class ratios
                "input": {
                    "type": "PREDICTIONS",
                    "name": "CLASS_DISTRIBUTION",
                    "task": task_name,
                },
                "strategy": {
                    "type": "BALANCE",
                    "target": {
                        dog: 0.50,
                        'sports ball': 0.50,
                    }
                },
            },
            {
                # strategy to use prediction score (Active
Learning)
                "input": {
                    "type": "SCORES",
                    "task": task_name,
                    "score": "object_frequency"
                },
                "strategy": {
                    "type": "WEIGHTS"
                },
            },
            {
                # strategy to use prediction score (Active
Learning)
                "input": {
                    "type": "SCORES",
                    "task": task_name,
                    "score": "objectness_least_confidence"
                },
                "strategy": {
                    "type": "WEIGHTS"
                },
            },
        ],
```

```
        },
        lightly_config={},
        runs_on=['Demo'],
    )
```

4. Now, organize the local files so that they match what Lightly is expecting:

```
!mkdir lightly && mkdir lightly/project_demo && mkdir lightly/
project_demo/.lightly
!mv metadata lightly/project_demo/.lightly && mv predictions
lightly/project_demo/.lightly
```

5. When we take a look at the folders, we'll see the following structure:

```
!ls lightly/project_demo/.lightly

metadata  predictions

!ls lightly/project_demo/.lightly/predictions/yolov8_demo_dog_detection

dog_running_ball-000-mp4.json   dog_running_ball-148-mp4.json
dog_running_ball-001-mp4.json   dog_running_ball-149-mp4.json
dog_running_ball-002-mp4.json   dog_running_ball-150-mp4.json
dog_running_ball-003-mp4.json   dog_running_ball-151-mp4.json
dog_running_ball-004-mp4.json   dog_running_ball-152-mp4.json
dog_running_ball-005-mp4.json   dog_running_ball-153-mp4.json
dog_running_ball-006-mp4.json   dog_running_ball-154-mp4.json
dog_running_ball-007-mp4.json   dog_running_ball-155-mp4.json
dog_running_ball-008-mp4.json   dog_running_ball-156-mp4.json
dog_running_ball-009-mp4.json   dog_running_ball-157-mp4.json
dog_running_ball-010-mp4.json   dog_running_ball-158-mp4.json
dog_running_ball-011-mp4.json   dog_running_ball-159-mp4.json
dog_running_ball-012-mp4.json   dog_running_ball-160-mp4.json
dog_running_ball-013-mp4.json   dog_running_ball-161-mp4.json
dog_running_ball-014-mp4.json   dog_running_ball-162-mp4.json
dog_running_ball-015-mp4.json   dog_running_ball-163-mp4.json
dog_running_ball-016-mp4.json   dog_running_ball-164-mp4.json
dog_running_ball-017-mp4.json   dog_running_ball-165-mp4.json
dog_running_ball-018-mp4.json   dog_running_ball-166-mp4.json

!ls videos/project_demo

dog_running_ball.mp4
```

Figure 5.4 – Folders organized for Lightly local storage

We are now ready to start the run.

Starting the worker and the active ML run

We need to create a function that will be used to initiate the worker with the organized folders that are mounted in the Docker container:

```
@contextlib.contextmanager
def start_worker(lightly_token, lightly_worker_id, image_
name="lightly/worker:latest", WORKER_LABEL="Demo") ->
Iterator[Container]:
    docker_client = docker.from_env()
    volumes = ["/home/user/videos:/input_mount",
               "/home/user/lightly:/lightly_mount"]
    container = docker_client.containers.run(
        image_name,
        f"token={lightly_token} worker.worker_id={lightly_worker_id}",
        detach=True,
        labels={"lightly_worker_label": WORKER_LABEL},
        volumes=volumes,
    )
    try:
        yield container
    finally:
        try:
            container.kill()
        except docker.errors.APIError:
            # if a container was killed from outside, we don't care
            pass
```

Let's start the run:

```
with start_worker(lightly_token, lightly_worker_id=worker_id):
    print('Worker running ...')
    last_run_info = None
    no_update_count = 0
    while True:
        run_info = client.get_compute_worker_run_info(
            scheduled_run_id=scheduled_run_id
        )
        print(run_info)
        if run_info.in_end_state():
            assert run_info.ended_successfully(),
                "Run did not end successfully"
            break
        if run_info != last_run_info:
            no_update_count = 0
```

```
    else:
        no_update_count += 1
        if no_update_count >= 10000:
            raise RuntimeError(
                f"Test timout: no run_info update\n"
                f"last_run_info: {str(last_run_info)},
                    run_info: {str(run_info)}"
            )
    last_run_info = run_info
```

We can check the progress of our run on the Lightly platform, as shown in *Figure 5.5*, as well as by looking at the output of the previous code:

Figure 5.5 – Lightly view of the active ML run

Once completed, we have access to a detailed report of the run and all the necessary logs, such as the memory log and default log. We can also view our dataset in the Lightly web application (`https://app.lightly.ai/dataset`).

Let's explore our results. In *Figure 5.6*, we can see that we have several new subfolders, including `frames` and `crops`. Those folders contain the selected frames and crops (cropped bounding boxes):

```
!ls lightly/project_demo/.lightly

crops  frames  metadata  predictions  runs  thumbnails

!ls lightly/project_demo/.lightly/frames

dog_running_ball-024-mp4.png  dog_running_ball-183-mp4.png
dog_running_ball-151-mp4.png  dog_running_ball-194-mp4.png
dog_running_ball-180-mp4.png
```

Figure 5.6 – Resulting folder after the Lightly active ML run

Let's visualize the selected frames:

```
most_informative_frames = glob('lightly/project_demo/.lightly/
frames/*.png')
for img_path in most_informative_frames:
    plt.imshow(Image.open(img_path))
    plt.show()
```

This returns the images shown in *Figure 5.7*:

Figure 5.7 – The five most informative frames that were chosen by the Lightly active ML run

We can also explore the report, which gives us a lot of information about our new subset of samples.

The report is saved under `lightly/project_demo/.lightly/runs/run_id`. We can view the run ID and then copy the `report.pdf` file locally, as shown in *Figure 5.8*:

```
!ls lightly/project_demo/.lightly/runs
65c12d12d17b6fe7d5c47631
!cp lightly/project_demo/.lightly/runs/65c12d12d17b6fe7d5c47631/report.pdf .
```

Figure 5.8 – Copying the report document

There is a lot of information in the report, so we will only focus on certain sections.

First, let's take a quick look at what we started with and what we ended up with. As shown in *Figure 5.9*, we had 290 frames and one video and created a subset of five frames only, which corresponds to our request for five samples. Note that the sample ratio can be selected with `n_samples`, but it can also be selected as a percentage of the data with `proportionSamples`. So, to select 30% of the data, we can set the following:

```
"proportionSamples": 0.30
```

We can do this instead of running the following:

```
"n_samples": 5
```

Here's the output:

Dataset Sizes

Metric	Image	Video
Input	290	1
Corrupt	0	0
Duplicate	0	0
Removed	285	1
Selected	5	1
Datapool Input	0	0
Datapool Selected	5	1

A video is considered {corrupt, ...} if it contains any {corrupt, ...} frames.

Figure 5.9 – Lightly report – dataset information

Now, let's examine the embeddings plots, as shown in *Figure 5.10*. Upon examining both the UMAP and PCA embeddings plots, we'll see the absence of distinct clusters, suggesting a lack of consistency among the frames. This inconsistency can be attributed to the video's dynamic filming conditions, including varying angles, distances to the dog, and changes in lighting due to shaded and non-shaded areas being encountered while moving around and following the dog. These factors contribute to the diverse visual input captured in the frames:

Image Level Analysis - Embeddings

Embedding 2D Scatter Plots

Two-dimensional scatter plots help to understand the distribution of the data and may enable quick insights about outlier cases, dataset bias, or class imbalances.

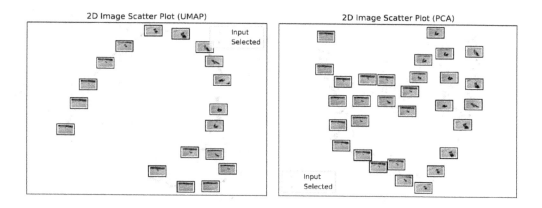

Figure 5.10 – Lightly report – embeddings plots

With *Figure 5.11*, we have a better understanding of which frames were selected by the active ML algorithm. We can see that it did a good job of selecting frames from diverse locations in the embeddings space:

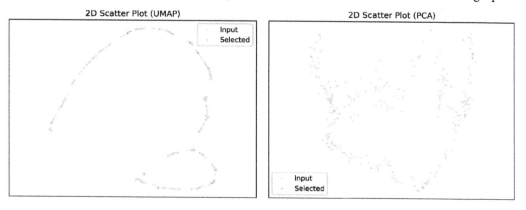

Figure 5.11 – Lightly report – embeddings plots selected frames

In *Figure 5.12*, we can observe that the class distribution has been effectively balanced: the dog class accounts for 54.5%, while the sports ball class accounts for 45.5% of the selection, closely aligning with our intended 50/50 class balance ratio. This balance was achieved thanks to our configured class balance ratios. Nonetheless, attaining such equilibrium often presents challenges, particularly when one class significantly outnumbers the others in the dataset:

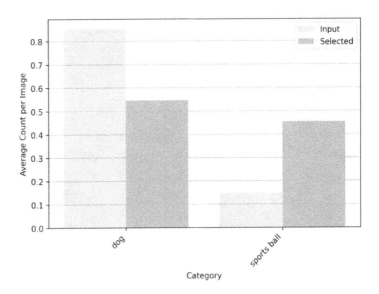

Category Distribution

Category	Input	Selected
dog	85.2%	54.5%
sports ball	14.8%	45.5%
All Categories	100%	100%

Figure 5.12 – Lightly report – class distribution

Now, we can explore some of the model predictions, as shown in *Figure 5.13*. Here, we have several examples of predictions with different numbers of detections. Overall, the model demonstrates strong performance, consistently identifying the dog within the frames. However, it appears to struggle more with detecting the ball. Notably, the ball was recognized in one of the sample frames, which is an encouraging sign. This discrepancy in detection accuracy likely comes from the nature of the ball used in the test; it deviates from the conventional sports balls, such as tennis or soccer balls, on which the original model was trained. This context helps explain the observed variations in model performance and can be fixed by labeling the ball and re-training the model:

Prediction Task: yolov8_demo_dog_detection

Figure 5.13 – Lightly report – examples of the model's predictions

Finally, *Figure 5.14* shows the selected frames throughout the video. Each selected frame corresponds to a vertical line, and we can confirm that there are five lines for our five selected frames:

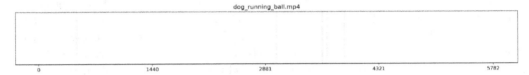

Figure 5.14 – Lightly report – video sampling densities

Now that we have the most informative frames we wish to label, we can send them to the annotation platform used in the project, such as Encord Annotate (https://docs.encord.com/docs/annotate-overview) or Roboflow (https://roboflow.com/), as presented in *Chapter 3, Managing the Human in the Loop*. In this example, we will use Encord Annotate because it offers a feature to visualize selected frames as videos.

Before running this code, you need to create an Encord SSH private key by following the documentation (https://docs.encord.com/reference/authentication-sdk) they provide.

Then, you can authenticate using the following code:

```
encord_private_key = "-----BEGIN OPENSSH PRIVATE KEY-----{your_key}---
--END OPENSSH PRIVATE KEY-----"
user_client = EncordUserClient.create_with_ssh_private_key(
    encord_private_key)
```

The next step is to create an Encord dataset (https://docs.encord.com/docs/annotate-datasets) with the name of our project – that is, project_demo. This Encord dataset is the data that we want to label:

```
print('\nCreating Encord Dataset...')
encord_dataset_created = user_client.create_dataset(
    'project_demo', StorageLocation.CORD_STORAGE
)
```

This will return a dictionary with the `title`, `type`, `dataset_hash`, `user_hash`, and `backing_folder_uuid` values of the created dataset. Here, we are using Encord's cloud storage, but you could also use custom cloud storage. For example, if you're using AWS S3, then you can use `StorageLocation.AWS` instead.

Now, we can query the dataset hash because it will be necessary when uploading the images:

```
dataset_hash = encord_dataset_created.dataset_hash
```

Next, we can populate the dataset with our selected frames:

```
dataset = user_client.get_dataset(dataset_hash)

image_files = sorted(
    [
        p.as_posix()
        for p in Path("lightly/project_demo/.lightly/frames").
iterdir()
        if p.suffix in {".jpg", ".png"}
    ]
)
dataset.create_image_group(image_files, create_video=True)
```

This will return a dictionary containing the `data_hash`, `backing_item_uuid`, and `title` values of the uploaded data.

Note that we used `create_video=True` so that we can create a compressed video from the image groups; these are called image sequences (https://docs.encord.com/docs/annotate-supported-data#image-sequences). This is beneficial when visualizing the frames as it helps maintain the temporal context of the videos and is usually very helpful for the labelers. It also allows the labelers to use features such as automated labeling (https://docs.encord.com/docs/automated-labeling), which includes interpolation. This helps speed up the labeling process considerably by automatically estimating the location of labels between two manually labeled frames.

At this point, we can view our dataset on the Encord web application, in the `Index/Datasets` section (`https://app.encord.com/datasets`), as shown in *Figure 5.15*. We can observe that the images are saved as `img_sequence`, which means that they will be displayed as a video:

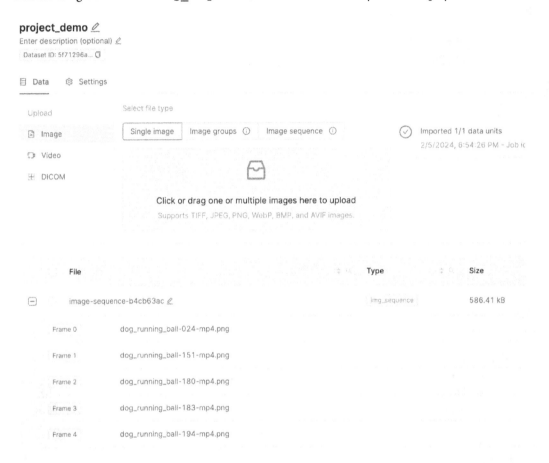

Figure 5.15 – Encord dataset with our five selected frames saved as an image sequence

In Encord, we define the ontology (`https://docs.encord.com/reference/ontologies-sdk`) that we want to use for this annotation project, as shown in *Figure 5.16*. We introduced the concept of ontologies in the *Designing interactive learning systems and workflows* section of *Chapter 3, Managing the Human in the Loop*:

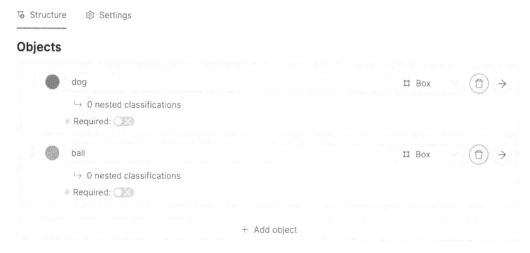

Figure 5.16 – Created ontology in Encord with our two classes, dog and ball

From the page visualized in *Figure 5.16*, we can copy the ontology ID and use it to create the Encord Annotate project (`https://docs.encord.com/docs/annotate-overview`):

```
project_hash = user_client.create_project(
        project_title='project_demo',
        dataset_hashes=[dataset_hash],
        ontology_hash='a0e16402-a5b4-417e-a4b1-7871ed386362')
```

We'll see the following:

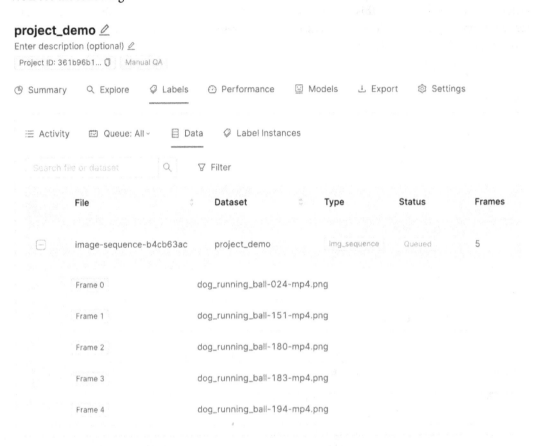

Figure 5.17 – Encord Annotate project of our project_demo samples

Our data is now ready to be labeled. We can view our Encord Annotate project in the `Annote/ Annotation projects` section (`https://app.encord.com/projects`) of the web app. Then, in the **Labels** section (see *Figure 5.17*) of our `project_demo` annotation project, we can view our selected frames as a video, as shown in *Figure 5.18*:

Figure 5.18 – Labeling view of the selected frames' image sequence in Encord

In the view presented in *Figure 5.18*, we can see that all the frames are presented as a video with a slider that the users can use to navigate the frames. There are also the two classes (dog and ball) that we defined in our ontology in the **Classes** section that labelers can select to label the frames, as shown in *Figure 5.19*:

Figure 5.19 – Example of annotations on one of the selected frames

From this page, labelers can use the automated labeling feature mentioned previously and easily label the objects; when they are done, they can submit the results for review.

You can also access the selected frames using the following code:

```
client_lightly_dataset = ApiWorkflowClient(
    token=lightly_token, dataset_id=dataset_id)
filenames_and_read_urls \
    client_lightly_dataset.export_filenames_and_read_urls_by_tag_name(
        tag_name="initial-tag"  # name of the tag in the dataset
)
print(f'There are {len(filenames_and_read_urls)} frames')
```

This returns the following output:

```
There are 5 frames
```

This is correct! Now, let's print the results so that we have a better understanding:

```
print(filenames_and_read_urls)
```

This returns the following output:

```
[{'fileName': 'dog_running_ball-024-mp4.png', 'readUrl': 'https://
api.lightly.ai/v1/datasets/...', 'datasourceUrl': 'project_demo/.
lightly/frames/dog_running_ball-024-mp4.png'}, .... {'fileName':
'dog_running_ball-180-mp4.png', 'readUrl': 'https://api.lightly.ai/
v1/datasets/...', 'datasourceUrl': 'project_demo/.lightly/frames/dog_
running_ball-180-mp4.png'}]
```

These URLs can be used to send the selected frames to the annotations platform used for the project. Note that since we are using local storage for the demo, the data isn't easily accessible to annotation platforms and cloud services should be used instead. The local data can also be visualized in Lightly by serving localhost (https://docs.lightly.ai/docs/local-storage#optional-view-local-data-in-lightly-platform).

In this section, we used Lightly to select the most informative frames in a test video of a dog running after a ball using several strategies. These strategies included finding diverse objects, balancing class ratios, using prediction scores for object frequencies, and considering the least confident results. Lightly has a lot of other features to improve these results and well-organized documentation (https://docs.lightly.ai/).

Next up, we will talk about how we can use Lightly for **self-supervised learning (SSL)**.

SSL with active ML

Lightly offers other useful features, such as **SSL**, which allows users to fine-tune an SSL model on their data before embedding the images. SSL algorithms exploit the structure and context within unlabeled images or videos to generate surrogate supervised signals that enable models to discover powerful visual representations on their own. For example, models may be trained to recognize spatial patterns, colorizations, rotations, or temporal ordering as pretext objectives before fine-tuning downstream tasks. In essence, SSL allows models to take advantage of vast volumes of unlabeled video and images to uncover useful features and patterns within the data itself, avoiding reliance on manual labeling, which can be infeasible at scale. The models automatically supervise their feature learning through carefully designed pretext tasks while harnessing aspects such as temporal continuity in a video. So, this Lightly feature can be extremely beneficial when developing models for a specific domain, such as medical videos. The additional training step improves the quality of the embeddings because the model can adapt to the specific domain without requiring more labeling.

Enabling SSL is simple and only requires adding a couple of lines to our code in the `worker_config` and `lightly_config` subdictionaries, both of which are part of the `scheduled_run_id` dictionary:

```
scheduled_run_id = client.schedule_compute_worker_run(
    worker_config={
        "enable_training": True
    },
    selection_config={
        "n_samples": 5,
        "strategies": [....], # same as before
    },
    lightly_config={
        'loader': {
            'num_workers': -1,
        },
        'trainer': {
            'max_epochs': 10,
            "gpus": 0, # cpu
        },
    },
    runs_on=['Demo'],
)
```

Here, we configured the active ML run to perform SSL training for 10 epochs on the CPU before generating the embeddings.

Now, let's take a look at our outputs. The frames that were selected are mostly different from the ones we selected previously – that is, dog_running_ball-024-mp4.png, dog_running_ball-101-mp4.png, dog_running_ball-033-mp4.png, dog_running_ball-224-mp4.png, and dog_running_ball-049-mp4.png – compared to dog_running_ball-024-mp4.png, dog_running_ball-183-mp4.png, dog_running_ball-151-mp4.png, dog_running_ball-194-mp4.png, and dog_running_ball-180-mp4.png.

So, only frame 024 was selected again. *Figure 5.20* shows the five most informative frames:

Figure 5.20 – Selecting the five most informative frames via a Lightly active ML SSL run

The frame that was selected in both the SSL and non-SSL runs is highlighted at the borders.

Figure 5.20 shows that the addition of the SSL step has noticeably altered the selection criteria for frames. Predominantly, frames chosen post-SSL tend to feature the dog at a further distance, contrasting sharply with those selected without SSL, which mainly consisted of close-ups showcasing the dog holding the ball. This shift underscores the impact of SSL on the model's focus and frame selection preferences:

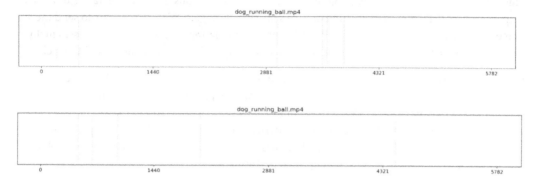

Figure 5.21 – Lightly report – comparing video sampling densities between the non-SSL run (top image) and the SSL run (bottom image)

Upon examining the new embedding plots shown in *Figure 5.21*, it is evident that the embeddings model performs better in clustering the frames. Despite this improvement, the clusters are not yet sharply defined, suggesting that extending the number of epochs in the SSL training could further refine this aspect:

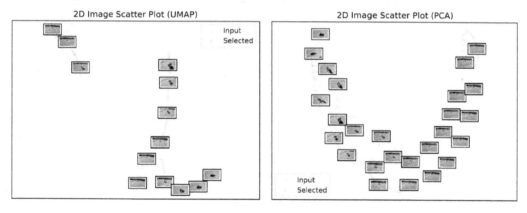

Figure 5.22 – New embeddings plots with the SSL active ML run

Incorporating the Lightly SSL feature into the ML pipeline is a straightforward addition that can provide significant benefits for field-specific data. By leveraging this advanced technique, we observed that the embeddings that were generated by the model were notably improved after undergoing SSL in our test. This enhancement not only enhances the overall performance but also ensures that the pipeline is optimized to handle the unique characteristics of the data being processed.

Summary

In this chapter, we learned how to use Lightly to efficiently select the most informative frames in videos to improve object detection models using diverse sampling strategies. We also saw how to send these selected frames to the labeling platform Encord, thereby completing an end-to-end use case. Finally, we explored how to further enhance sampling by incorporating an SSL step into the active ML pipeline.

Moving forward, our focus will shift to exploring how to effectively evaluate, monitor, and test the active ML pipeline. This step is essential in ensuring that the pipeline remains robust and reliable throughout its deployment. By implementing comprehensive evaluation strategies, we can assess the performance of the pipeline against predefined metrics and benchmarks. Additionally, continuous monitoring will allow us to identify any potential issues or deviations from expected behavior, enabling us to take proactive measures to maintain optimal performance.

Furthermore, rigorous testing of the active ML pipeline is essential to verify its functionality and validate its accuracy. Through systematic testing procedures, we can ensure that the pipeline behaves consistently under various scenarios and input conditions. This will involve designing and executing diverse test cases that cover a wide range of potential use cases and edge scenarios.

By thoroughly evaluating, monitoring, and testing the active ML pipeline, we can instill confidence in its reliability and performance. This robust framework will enable us to make informed decisions and drive valuable insights from the processed data, ultimately leading to improved outcomes and enhanced decision-making capabilities in the field-specific domain.

Part 3:
Applying Active Machine Learning to Real-World Projects

Part 3 concludes the exploration of active **machine learning (ML)** by equipping readers with the knowledge to not only understand advanced active ML methods but also to apply them effectively in real-world scenarios. Through the advanced tools discussed in these chapters, practitioners will be prepared to tackle complex challenges, drive innovation, and achieve significant improvements in their ML projects. Whether it's through refining evaluation practices or leveraging powerful software, this section aims to inspire and guide readers toward mastery of the art and science of active ML.

This part includes the following chapters:

- *Chapter 6, Evaluating and Enhancing Efficiency*
- *Chapter 7, Utilizing Tools and Packages for Active ML*

6

Evaluating and Enhancing Efficiency

In this chapter, we will explore the important aspects of rigorously evaluating the performance of active machine learning systems. We will cover various topics such as automation, testing, monitoring, and determining the stopping criteria. In this chapter we will use a paid cloud service, such as AWS, to demonstrate how an automatic, efficient active learning pipeline can be implemented in the real world.

By thoroughly understanding these concepts and techniques, we can ensure a comprehensive active ML process that yields accurate and reliable results. Through this exploration, we will gain insights into the effectiveness and efficiency of active ML systems, enabling us to make informed decisions and improvements.

By the end of this chapter, we will have covered the following:

- Creating efficient active ML pipelines
- Monitoring active ML pipelines
- Determining when to stop active ML runs
- Enhancing production model monitoring with active ML

Technical requirements

For this chapter, you will need the following:

- A MongoDB account: (https://www.mongodb.com/)
- A ClearML account: (https://app.clear.ml/)
- GPU: You may check out the specific hardware requirements from the web page of the tool you will be using
- An EC2 instance, factoring in cost considerations

In this chapter, you will need to install these packages:

```
pip install clearml
pip install pymongo
```

You will need the following imports:

```
import os
from clearml import Task, TaskTypes
import pymongo
import datetime
```

Creating efficient active ML pipelines

As we have seen in the previous chapter, efficient active ML pipelines consist of end-to-end pipelines. This means that the active ML algorithm needs to be able to access the unlabeled data, select the most informative frames, and then seamlessly send them to the labeling platform. All these steps need to happen one after the other in an automatic manner in order to reduce manual intervention.

Moreover, it is essential to test this pipeline to ensure that each step works properly. An example of a cloud-hosted active ML pipeline would be as follows:

1. Unlabeled data is stored in an AWS S3 bucket.

2. An active ML algorithm runs on an EC2 instance that can access the S3 bucket.

3. The results of the active ML run are saved in a dedicated S3 bucket specifically for this purpose and are linked to the labeling platform used for the project.

4. The final step of the active ML run is to link the selected frames to the labeling platform and create the annotation project, ready for the labelers to work on it.

When selecting and configuring the EC2 instance for running the active ML code, it is essential to consider efficiency. It is highly likely that a GPU will be required to perform the inference and compute the active ML embeddings. For example, if you are using Lightly, you can refer to their hardware recommendations on this page (https://docs.lightly.ai/docs/hardware-recommendations). Additionally, it is important to take into account the cost of the chosen EC2 instance and determine if it aligns with your budget. You can find the AWS EC2 on-demand pricing here (https://aws.amazon.com/ec2/pricing/on-demand/). When you are not running any active ML process, stopping the instance is a good practice to save money.

Other good practices include having a requirements.txt file that lists all the required versions of the packages for the run. For example, for the packages used in *Chapter 5*, *Leveraging Active Learning for Big Data*, the `requirements.txt` file would look something like this.

```
awscli==1.31.6
ultralytics==8.0.145
lightly==1.4.23
docker==6.1.3
encord==0.1.85
```

You can replace any version with the desired version; ideally, using the latest versions of the packages would be better.

Additionally, making the pipeline configurable through parameters enables easier scaling. For example, specifying options such as sampling strategy, model selection, and data source via a YAML configuration file. This allows for changing pipeline behavior without code changes, simplifying integration into workflows. As a reminder, we have explored different sampling strategies in *Chapter 2*, *Designing Query Strategy Frameworks*, and we have explored model selection for computer vision tasks in *Chapter 4*, *Applying Active Learning to Computer Vision*.

A simple example of configuring a YAML file using our Lightly example from *Chapter 5*, *Leveraging Active Learning for Big Data*, might look like this:

```
model_path_in_s3: 's3://my-models-library/my-best-object-detection-
model.pt'
inference_confidence_threshold: 0.3
proportionSamples: 0.20  # 20% of the samples
isSSLenabled: true
maxSSLepochs: 20
important_classes: {"person": 0, " sports ball": 32}
balance: true
balance_strategy:{ 'person': 0.50, 'sports ball': 0.50}
videos_folder_in_s3: "test"
s3_bucket_output: 'labeling-queue'
```

Then, those parameters can be accessed using this function:

```
def get_config_yaml(path_to_config_yaml="config.yaml"):
    # Open the YAML file
    with open(path_to_config_yaml, "r") as file:
        # Load the YAML content
        config = yaml.safe_load(file)
    file.close()
    return config
```

Followed by this:

```
config = get_config_yaml(path_to_config_yaml="config.yaml")
model_path_in_s3 = config["model_path_in_s3"]
inference_confidence_threshold = config["inference_confidence_
threshold"]
proportionSamples = config["proportionSamples"]
isSSLenabled = config["isSSLenabled"]
if isSSLenabled:
  maxSSLepochs = config['maxSSLepochs']

important_classes = config["important_classes"]
s3_bucket_output = config["s3_bucket_output"]

balance_strategy = config['balance_strategy']
if balance_strategy:
  balance = config['balance']
```

Those variables can then be used in the code in *Chapter 5, Leveraging Active Learning for Big Data*, and will make it scalable to all workflows and applications.

Thus, for your projects, you only need to change the YAML file and can then use the scripts for all your projects without modifying the scripts themselves.

Next, we will explore solutions to monitor our active ML runs and make sure that we are able to have a full overview of the whole process.

Monitoring active ML pipelines

The **proactive monitoring** of active ML pipelines is critical to ensure their optimal performance in production environments. Achieving this requires a focused approach on several key areas for effective observation, utilizing a variety of specialized tools specifically designed for these tasks. A central aspect of this monitoring process is **comprehensive logging**. It is essential for every phase of the active ML pipeline to implement detailed logging practices, capturing a broad spectrum of data, such as useful insights, errors, warnings, and other pertinent metadata. This diligent approach to log monitoring is key in quickly identifying and diagnosing issues, enabling prompt and efficient resolutions. Furthermore, these logs offer invaluable insights into the pipeline's performance and behavior, aiding in the continuous enhancement of the active ML systems. Simple logging can be done in the scripts themselves with libraries such as `logging`, which is a versatile and built-in library.

Incorporating an MLOps platform such as **ClearML** (`https://clear.ml/`) can significantly streamline the monitoring of pipeline runs. ClearML provides real-time statistics, graphical data visualizations, extensive logging, model artifacts, and the ability to compare pipeline runs in a side-by-side format. While traditionally used for improving the observability of ML training and deployment pipelines, ClearML is also highly effective for active ML pipelines, enhancing their management and oversight.

The following sample code snippet can be seamlessly integrated into the active ML codebase. This snippet is designed to set up a ClearML project named `active_learning_runs` and initialize a task within it, labeled `testing-AL`, which corresponds to a specific run. Once implemented, this configuration enables the automatic tracking of the run, as illustrated in *Figure 6.1*, under the console tab of the ClearML project configured via this code snippet:

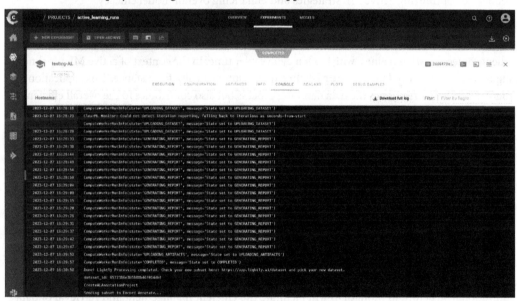

Figure 6.1 – Console log automatically saved after initializing the ClearML run

This integration not only streamlines the process of monitoring and managing ML runs but also ensures that all relevant data and metrics are systematically captured and made accessible for analysis within the ClearML platform:

```
Task.set_credentials(api_host='https://api.community.clear.ml',
                     web_host='https://app.community.clear.ml',
                     key='your_clearml_access_key',
                     secret='your_clearml_secret_key')
task = Task.init(project_name='active_learning_runs',
                 task_name='testing-AL',
                 task_type=TaskTypes.inference)
```

We opt for the ClearML task type `TaskTypes.inference`, as it is specifically tailored to facilitate the comprehensive logging and meticulous monitoring of the inference processes in machine learning. This task type is adept at meticulously tracking the input data, the predictions outputted by the model, and a range of relevant metrics or performance indicators, making it particularly suited for active ML runs. Indeed, as we have seen in previous chapters, active ML runs consist of conducting inference to identify the most advantageous frames to add to the labeling queue. Therefore, `TaskTypes.inference` is the ideal choice here. This task type is instrumental in enabling the systematic collection and thorough analysis of key performance metrics unique to the inference stage, such as latency. Furthermore, utilizing `TaskTypes.inference` empowers teams to accrue critical insights regarding the model's behavior when interfacing with real-time data—a fundamental aspect for the success of active ML systems. This detailed understanding of a run's real-time performance is invaluable for optimizing active ML strategies and enhancing overall model efficacy.

Another valuable tool for monitoring active ML pipelines is **MongoDB** (https://www.mongodb.com/), which is a widely used database known for its user-friendly nature. Its flexibility makes it an excellent choice for ML pipelines, which often evolve over time. In the context of active ML pipelines, MongoDB can be employed to generate a labeling queue automatically, for instance. This application of MongoDB not only streamlines the data handling process but also contributes to the overall efficiency and adaptability of the ML pipeline.

Let's take a look at an example code snippet for this. First, we need to log in to mongodb:

```
username = 'your_mongodb_username'
password = 'your_mongodb_pwd'
cluster = 'your_mongodb_cluster'
uri = 'mongodb+srv://' + username + ':' + password + '@' + cluster
client = pymongo.MongoClient(uri)
```

Next, we create a MongoDB collection specifically for this project, which we will name `ml_demo_project`. Within this collection, we will create a table titled `ml_labeling_queue_demo`. This organizational structure in MongoDB will facilitate the efficient management and retrieval of data pertinent to our project:

```
db = client['ml_demo_project']
collection = db['ml_labeling_queue_demo']
```

The final step involves populating our labeling queue table with data derived from our active ML run. This is a general example and should be tailored to fit the specific requirements of individual projects. By integrating this step, we ensure that the information from the ML run is accurately and efficiently transferred to the labeling queue, setting the stage for subsequent processing and analysis tailored to the unique needs of each project:

```
document = {'Name dataset': 'demo',
            'Labeler': 'TBD',
            'Reviewer': 'TBD',
```

```
                'Labeling status': 'In queue',
                'Reviewing status': 'None',
                'date': datetime.datetime.now()}
    collection.insert_one(document)
```

This MongoDB collection streamlines the process of monitoring progress in the labeling queue, facilitating efficient communication with labelers about upcoming items. This setup eliminates the need for the manual entry of each new annotation project, significantly enhancing workflow efficiency. By automating the tracking and updating of the queue, it ensures a more seamless and coordinated approach to managing labeling tasks.

Actively monitoring via logs, MLOps platforms, databases, and other tools is essential for maintaining visibility and quickly catching any issues in production-active ML pipelines. This helps minimize risks and improve system reliability.

To ensure that this monitoring is effectively utilized in decision-making processes, it's crucial to establish clear criteria for critical actions, such as determining when to stop active ML runs, which we will cover next.

Determining when to stop active ML runs

Active ML runs are dynamic and iterative processes that require careful monitoring, as we have already seen. But they also require strategic decision-making to determine the optimal point for cessation. The decision to stop an active ML run is critical as it impacts both the performance and efficiency of the learning model. This section focuses on the key considerations and strategies to effectively determine when to stop active machine learning runs.

In active ML, establishing clear performance goals specific to the project is crucial. For instance, consider a project aimed at developing a facial recognition system. Here, accuracy and precision might be the chosen performance metrics. A diverse test set, mirroring real-world conditions and varied facial features, is crucial for evaluating the model.

Let's say the pre-defined threshold on the established test set for accuracy is set at 95% and for precision, at 90%. The active ML process should continue until the model consistently achieves or surpasses these metrics on the test set. If the model shows an accuracy of 95% or more and a precision of 90% or more on the test set, it suggests the model has learned to generalize well across different faces and scenarios. This consistent performance on a diverse test set indicates the model is ready for real-world application, having been effectively tailored through the active learning process.

Additional considerations play a vital role in determining when to stop the active ML process. In the preceding facial recognition example, there are several simple but important additional factors to consider when deciding to stop the active ML process. Here are some steps you could take before deciding to stop the active ML process:

- **Watch out for overfitting**: This happens when the model does much better on training data than on the test set. If we see this, it's time to stop and adjust the model to avoid overfitting.

- **Think about our resources**: Resources such as time, computing power, and money are scarce. Even if our model hasn't hit the 95% accuracy or 90% precision we want, we might have to stop if we're running low on these resources.

- **Be aware of diminishing returns**: This means if training more isn't really improving our model, it might have learned as much as it can. Continuing to train it in this case won't help.

- **Keep reassessing the model with feedback loops**: As the world and data change, our model's goals might need to change, too. Regularly checking that our model still meets our current needs helps keep it relevant and effective.

The decision to stop an active ML run should be based on a combination of reaching predefined performance metrics, maintaining stability on a diverse test set, monitoring resource constraints, and being vigilant about overfitting and diminishing returns. By carefully considering these factors, we can ensure that active ML models are both effective and efficient, aligning with the overarching goals of the project.

Let's now discuss how we can use active learning in a production environment.

Enhancing production model monitoring with active ML

Having already established a comprehensive understanding of active ML, this section shifts focus to its practical application in monitoring machine learning models in production environments. The dynamic nature of user data and market conditions presents a unique challenge for maintaining the accuracy and relevance of deployed models. Active ML emerges as a pivotal tool in this context, offering a proactive approach to identify and adapt to changes in real time. This section will explore the methodologies and strategies through which active ML can be harnessed to continuously improve and adjust models based on evolving user data, ensuring that these models remain robust, efficient, and aligned with current trends and user behaviors.

Challenges in monitoring production models

There are several challenges when it comes to monitoring production models. First, we have data drift and model decay.

Data drift refers to the change in the input data fed into a machine learning model over time. This change can occur due to various reasons, such as evolving user behaviors, seasonal effects, economic shifts, or changes in the broader environment in which the model operates. The key characteristic of data drift is that the statistical properties of the current input data differ from those of the original training data, as shown in *Figure 6.2*. Data drift can significantly impact the performance of a model since the assumptions the model was originally trained on no longer hold true. It can lead to a decrease in accuracy and reliability, making the model less effective at making predictions or classifications:

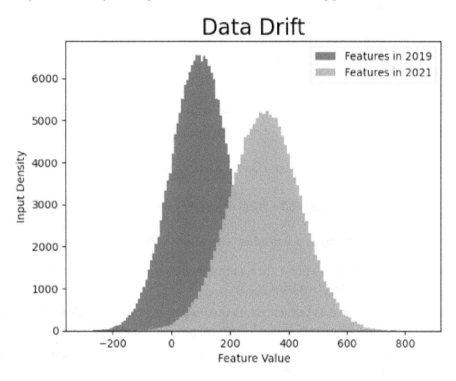

Figure 6.2 – Illustration of data drift

Model decay, also known as model degradation or performance decay, refers to the decline in the performance of a machine learning model over time. This phenomenon is closely related to data drift, as shown in *Figure 6.3*, as one of the primary causes of model decay is the changing nature of the data the model encounters in a live environment:

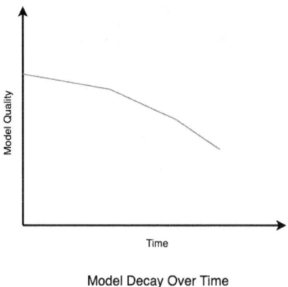

Figure 6.3 – Model decay over time

However, model decay can also occur due to other factors, such as the following:

- **Changes in relationships**: Over time, the relationships between variables might change, making the model's learned patterns outdated

- **Feedback loops**: If a model's predictions are used as part of a decision-making process that influences future data, it can create feedback loops that gradually degrade the model's performance

- **External factors**: Unforeseen external factors such as policy changes, natural disasters, or global events can also lead to model decay

Both data drift and model decay highlight the need for continuous monitoring and updating machine learning models in production. Identifying when and how these changes occur is crucial for maintaining the effectiveness and accuracy of the models.

Active ML to monitor models in production

Active ML is particularly well suited to combat data drift and model decay due to its dynamic and responsive nature. Indeed, active ML stands out for its targeted data acquisition, as previously discussed in our chapters, where it excels in identifying and acquiring the most informative data points. This approach is particularly advantageous in addressing data drift and model decay, as the algorithm actively queries for new data that accurately represents the current environment or user behavior. This method is not only more efficient than passively collecting large datasets but also ensures that the data is relevant and not redundant. Active ML systems are inherently adaptable, quickly adjusting their understanding and predictions in response to new data, a feature crucial for maintaining effectiveness amidst changing data distributions. This adaptability is augmented by the system's capacity for continuous learning and improvement. As active ML systems receive new data points and feedback, they are constantly updating and refining their models, thereby mitigating the effects of model decay and ensuring that the models evolve in line with changes in the data and environment.

Active ML addresses the cost and time-intensive nature of data labeling by selecting the most informative samples, a process that proves especially beneficial in adapting to data drift. The efficient use of resources in labeling ensures maximum benefit to the model. Additionally, active ML algorithms are designed for the **early detection of shifts in data patterns** or **performance drops**, acting as an early warning system for data drift and model decay. This early detection capability allows for prompt interventions, such as model adjustments or retraining, to prevent significant performance degradation.

In *Chapter 2*, *Designing Query Strategy Frameworks*, we also discussed how active ML provides customizable query strategies, including uncertainty sampling and query by committee, which can be tailored to the specific needs of an application. This flexibility enables more effective responses to the unique challenges of data drift and model decay in various scenarios, underlining the comprehensive adaptability of active ML in dynamic data environments.

The early detection of drift and decay is crucial to sustain the performance of machine learning models once they are deployed. Active ML assumes an indispensable role here, functioning effectively as an early warning system. This capability is crucial for the pre-emptive identification and mitigation of potential issues before they escalate, thus preserving the model's integrity and accuracy.

We will now explore the mechanisms and strategies through which active ML can be used to accomplish this, highlighting its significance in the proactive management and maintenance of ML models in dynamic environments.

Here are some mechanisms for early detection using active ML methods that we have seen in previous chapters:

1. **Uncertainty sampling**: Active ML algorithms often employ uncertainty sampling, where the model identifies data points for which it has the lowest confidence in its predictions. A sudden increase in the number of such points can signal a change in the underlying data distribution, indicating potential data drift.

2. **Anomaly detection**: Active ML systems can be equipped with anomaly detection capabilities to spot unusual patterns in incoming data. These anomalies might be indicative of changes in the data landscape that could lead to model decay if not addressed.

3. **Query by committee**: This approach involves maintaining multiple models or versions of a model (the committee) and using their disagreement to identify challenging data points. A growing disparity in the predictions of committee members can indicate emerging data drift or model decay, as it suggests that the models are becoming increasingly uncertain about the current data.

4. **Feedback loops**: In scenarios where user feedback or real-world outcomes are available, active ML can use this feedback to assess model performance. Rapid changes in user feedback patterns can provide early indications of shifts in data trends or declining model effectiveness.

Active ML's capability for early issue detection is essential, allowing for prompt and timely interventions. This proactive strategy is markedly more effective than conventional reactive methods, where issues are only addressed following notable performance declines. By identifying problems early, active ML ensures that resources allocated for model retraining or adjustments are utilized efficiently and judiciously. This aspect is particularly crucial in environments where computational resources or labeled data are scarce. Moreover, in end-user applications, the consistency of model performance is essential for maintaining user trust. Through the early detection and timely correction of data drift or model decay, active ML contributes significantly to a reliable and consistent user experience, underlining its value in sustaining the credibility and effectiveness of machine learning models in various real-world applications.

Early detection for data drift and model decay

The effective implementation of early detection for data drift and model decay in active ML necessitates several key considerations:

- Choosing the right metrics for monitoring is the key. The metrics should align closely with the model's objectives and the unique characteristics of the data and application.

- Setting realistic thresholds for alerts is also crucial, striking a balance between sensitivity and practicality to avoid frequent false alarms or missing critical changes.

- Integrating active ML systems with existing data pipelines is crucial for real-time monitoring and quick responses to detected issues, thereby enhancing system efficiency and responsiveness. For practical implementation, this means linking the active ML algorithm directly to the storage of user data, enabling the system to engage and analyze new data automatically as soon as it's uploaded. This integration ensures continuous, up-to-date monitoring, which is vital for the timely detection and handling of potential data drift or model decay.

Let's consider an example from a retail use case, specifically in the context of a computer vision system used for inventory management. Imagine a retail store using an active ML system equipped with computer vision for inventory management. This system is designed to monitor the store's shelves using cameras to track stock levels, detect when items are running low, and identify when restocking is needed. The computer vision model is initially trained on a dataset of images depicting various states of shelf stock, from fully stocked to nearly empty. It learns to recognize different products, their locations, and their quantities. Over time, the store introduces new products and changes the layout of some items. The active ML system, during its routine monitoring, starts detecting anomalies in the images; the model encounters unfamiliar images, leading to uncertainty in its predictions. This uncertainty, often reflected in lower confidence scores, indicates potential anomalies. The system also employs statistical methods to identify outliers—data points that significantly deviate from established patterns of product arrangements. Additionally, it analyzes changes over time, comparing current images against historical data to spot deviations in product types or arrangements. When the system flags an anomaly, it alerts store managers for further inspection. If the change is intentional, such as with the introduction of new products, this information is used to update and retrain the model, ensuring it adapts to the new store layout and inventory. If the change is unintentional, such as a misplaced product, it can be corrected to maintain inventory accuracy. This adaptive process ensures the ML model remains effective in real-time inventory management, adjusting to both gradual and sudden changes in the retail environment.

In this example, the active ML system's anomaly detection capability is crucial for maintaining the effectiveness of the inventory management system. It ensures that the computer vision model remains accurate and reliable in tracking inventory despite changes in the store's product range and layout, thus preventing model decay and ensuring operational efficiency.

To sum up, by focusing on the most informative data points and integrating user feedback, active ML provides a dynamic approach to maintaining the relevance and accuracy of models amidst evolving user data and market conditions. The adaptability and efficiency delivered by this approach are vital for the long-term success of machine learning applications in various sectors.

Summary

In this chapter, we have delved deeply into the crucial aspects of rigorously evaluating the performance of active ML systems. We began by understanding the significance of automating processes to enhance efficiency and accuracy. The chapter then guided us through various testing methodologies, emphasizing their role in ensuring robust and reliable active ML pipelines.

A significant portion of our discussion focused on the criticality of the continuous monitoring of active ML pipelines. This monitoring is not just about observing the performance but also involves understanding and interpreting the results to make data-driven decisions.

One of the most pivotal topics we covered was determining the appropriate stopping criteria for active ML runs. We explored how setting pre-defined performance metrics, such as accuracy and precision, is crucial in guiding these decisions. We also emphasized the importance of a diverse and representative test set to ensure the model's applicability in real-world scenarios.

Additionally, we discussed the need to be mindful of overfitting, resource limitations, diminishing returns, and the importance of implementing feedback loops. These considerations play a key role in not only determining when to stop the ML run but also in ensuring the overall success and relevance of the model in a constantly evolving environment.

Finally, we have established that active ML is exceptionally adept at monitoring models in production environments. Its application extends to the early detection of data drift and model decay, particularly when seamlessly integrated into user data pipelines. This integration enables the active ML system to monitor data, ensuring that any deviations or anomalies are promptly detected continuously. Moreover, the system can be configured to trigger alerts when these irregularities occur, allowing for immediate attention and action. This capability not only enhances the model's reliability and accuracy but also ensures its adaptability and resilience in the face of evolving data landscapes, making active ML a powerful tool in production model monitoring.

In the next chapter, *Utilizing Tools and Packages for Active ML*, we will turn our attention to the various Python libraries, frameworks, and tools commonly used in active ML. We will provide an overview of these resources, highlighting their value in implementing various active ML techniques. This will equip you with the necessary knowledge and skills to elevate your active ML projects and define what tools are best suited for them. This chapter promises to be a comprehensive guide to the current active ML tools.

7

Utilizing Tools and Packages for Active ML

In this chapter, we will discuss a range of Python libraries, frameworks, and tools commonly used in active ML. These resources are instrumental to implementing a variety of active ML techniques. The content of this chapter is structured to be informative and useful for individuals at different levels of expertise, from beginners to experienced programmers. The aim is to provide a solid understanding of the tools we will cover in order to effectively incorporate active ML techniques into your projects.

Throughout this chapter, the focus will be on understanding Python packages for active ML. We will use the popular Python libraries scikit-learn and modAL. You'll learn about their functionalities and how they can be applied to active ML scenarios. We will also explore a range of active ML tools. In addition to the tools covered in previous sections of the book, this chapter will introduce some additional active ML tools. Each tool will be presented with an overview of its features and potential applications, helping you to understand how they fit into different active ML contexts.

In this chapter, we will discuss the following topics:

- Mastering Python packages for enhanced active ML
- Getting familiar with the active ML tools

Technical requirements

For the exercises in this chapter, you will need to install these packages:

```
pip install scikit-learn
pip install modAL-python
```

And you will need the following imports:

```
from sklearn.cluster import KMeans
from sklearn.linear_model import LogisticRegression
```

```
from sklearn.utils import shuffle
import numpy as np
import random
from modAL.models import ActiveLearner, Committee
from sklearn.ensemble import RandomForestClassifier
from modAL.uncertainty import uncertainty_sampling
import os
from PIL import Image
from sklearn.model_selection import train_test_split
import matplotlib.pyplot as plt
from sklearn.datasets import load_iris
from modAL.disagreement import vote_entropy_sampling
```

Mastering Python packages for enhanced active ML

This section offers a comprehensive overview of two popular Python packages known for their capabilities in facilitating active ML: **scikit-learn** and **modAL**. scikit-learn, a versatile and user-friendly library, is foundational in the ML community for its extensive array of traditional ML tools. On the other hand, modAL, specifically designed for active ML, builds upon scikit-learn's robust framework to introduce more dynamic, data-efficient learning techniques. Together, these packages represent a powerful toolkit for anyone looking to leverage the strengths of active ML methodologies.

scikit-learn

While not exclusively for active ML, **scikit-learn** (https://scikit-learn.org/stable/index.html) is a foundational package in Python's machine learning ecosystem. It offers a broad range of algorithms and tools that are often used in conjunction with active ML packages – a vast collection of algorithms for classification, regression, clustering, and dimensionality reduction. It also provides tools for model evaluation and data preprocessing.

scikit-learn is typically used as a base for model development and is often integrated with active ML packages for model training and evaluation.

For instance, scikit-learn can be used to perform customer segmentation in marketing by clustering customers based on purchasing behavior, demographics, and engagement metrics. K-means clustering, a popular algorithm in scikit-learn, helps in identifying distinct customer groups for targeted marketing campaigns. Active ML can be incorporated by iteratively refining the clustering model. For instance, marketing analysts can label ambiguous cases where the clustering algorithm is uncertain, improving the model's accuracy over time.

Let's illustrate this with a simulated example.

First, we perform the initial clustering with KMeans. We start by defining some mock customer data (age, annual income):

```
X = np.array([[34, 20000], [42, 30000], [23, 25000], [32, 45000],
    [38, 30000]])
```

Then we use KMeans for clustering:

```
kmeans = KMeans(n_clusters=2, random_state=0).fit(X)
```

And we predict the cluster for each customer:

```
clusters = kmeans.predict(X)
```

We have segmented our customers into two clusters based on age and annual income.

Next, we set up the active ML section. Let's assume that we have a larger, unlabeled dataset of customer features called X_unlabeled. In the context of our customer segmentation scenario using KMeans, unlabeled data would consist of customer records with the same features we used for clustering (in our case, age and annual income), but without any assigned cluster labels. This data is what we'll use to apply and refine our clustering and classification models in an active ML framework:

```
X_unlabeled = np.array([[28, 22000], [45, 55000], [37, 35000],
    [50, 48000], [29, 27000], [41, 32000]])
```

We need a model (a classifier) to make predictions on this unlabeled data. Let's use a simple classifier called LogisticRegression for illustration. We initialize this classifier and use the clusters as labels to train it on our initial dataset (X):

```
classifier = LogisticRegression()
classifier.fit(X, clusters)
```

Then we implement the active ML loop. In each iteration, the classifier predicts labels for the unlabeled data. First, we need to create a obtain_labels placeholder function where we obtain the true labels for the selected data points. In a real-world scenario, this function would involve a process to acquire the actual labels, such as conducting surveys or expert analysis. Since we're creating a simulated example, we design this function to randomly assign labels based on some assumed logic:

```
def obtain_labels(data):
    return np.random.choice([0, 1], size=len(data))
```

For our active ML loop, we need to choose how many iterations we want to go through and how many samples will be labeled in each iteration:

```
num_iterations = 10
num_to_label = 2
```

We can now create our active ML loop that will do the following:

1. Select instances for which the classifier is least confident.

2. Obtain true labels for these instances (in practice, this might involve manual labeling or additional data collection).

3. Update the classifier with these new labels.

4. Periodically update the KMeans model with the newly labeled data to refine the customer segments.

The following is a code snippet that helps us to achieve this:

```
for iteration in range(num_iterations):
    if len(X_unlabeled) == 0:
        break  # No more data to label

    # Predict on unlabeled data
    predictions = classifier.predict_proba(X_unlabeled)
    uncertainty = np.max(predictions, axis=1)

    # Select num_to_label instances with least confidence
    uncertain_indices = np.argsort(uncertainty)[:num_to_label]

    # Obtain labels for these instances
    new_labels = obtain_labels(X_unlabeled[uncertain_indices])

    # Update our dataset
    X = np.vstack([X, X_unlabeled[uncertain_indices]])
    clusters = np.hstack([clusters, new_labels])

    # Re-train classifier and KMeans
    classifier.fit(X, clusters)
    kmeans.fit(X)

    print(f"Iteration {iteration+1}, Labeled Data: {
        X_unlabeled[uncertain_indices]} with Labels: {new_labels}")

    # Remove labeled instances from unlabeled data
    X_unlabeled = np.delete(X_unlabeled, uncertain_indices, axis=0)

    # Shuffle unlabeled data to avoid any order bias
    X_unlabeled = shuffle(X_unlabeled)
```

The preceding code returns the following:

```
Iteration 1, Labeled Data: [[45 55000] [29 27000]] with Labels: [0 1]
Iteration 2, Labeled Data: [[37 35000] [28 22000]] with Labels: [1 1]
Iteration 3, Labeled Data: [[41 32000] [50 48000]] with Labels: [0 0]
```

Our active ML loop iterates a specified number of times, each time selecting the least confident predictions made by the classifier, obtaining labels for these instances, and then updating the classifier and KMeans model with the new data. Remember, the obtain_labels function is a simplification. In a real application, obtaining labels would involve an oracle manually labeling the samples as we described in *Chapter 3, Managing the Human in the Loop*.

modAL

modAL (https://modal-python.readthedocs.io/en/latest/) is a modular and flexible active ML framework built on top of scikit-learn. It allows for easy integration of active learning strategies into existing ML workflows. It provides various active ML strategies such as uncertainty sampling and query by committee. It also supports custom query strategies and easy integration with scikit-learn models.

For example, it is ideal for tasks such as image classification and regression where active ML can efficiently select informative samples for annotation.

Let's take a look at an example where we classify images from the popular **CIFAR10** dataset. This dataset can be loaded from built-in torchvision datasets. Given the large volume of images, active ML can help prioritize which images should be labeled manually. We will use the modAL framework's uncertainty sampling query strategy. It will be able to identify the most informative images (those where the classifier is most uncertain) and query them for labeling.

We implement a load_images function to read images from the dataset directory, then we convert them to grayscale and flatten the images for training. Indeed, we need to transform the image data into a format compatible with RandomForest, so each image, which is a 2D array, is *flattened* into a 1D array. This means converting the image into a long vector of pixel values. For our grayscale images of size 32x32 pixels, the flattened form will be a vector of 1,024 elements (32x32):

```python
def load_data():
    # Define the transformation
    transform = transforms.Compose([
        transforms.ToTensor(),  # Convert images to PyTorch tensors
    ])
        # Load the CIFAR10 dataset
```

```
    dataset = CIFAR10(root='data', train=True, download=True,
        transform=transform)

    # Load all data into memory (for small datasets)
    dataloader = DataLoader(dataset, batch_size=len(dataset),
        shuffle=False)
    data_iter = iter(dataloader)
    images, labels = next(data_iter)

    # Convert images and labels to numpy arrays
    X_all = images.numpy()
    y_all = np.array(labels)

    # Convert images from 3D to 1D (batch_size, 3, 32, 32) -> (batch_
size, 3072) for RandomForest
    X_all = X_all.reshape(X_all.shape[0], -1)

    # Map numerical labels to string labels
    class_names = dataset.classes
    y_all = np.array([class_names[label] for label in y_all])

    return X_all, y_all
```

Next, for our example, we split the dataset into initial labeled data with the images stored in X_initial and the labels stored in y_initial and unlabeled data as X_unlabeled:

```
X_initial, X_unlabeled, y_initial, _ = train_test_split(X_all, y_all,
    test_size=0.75, random_state=42)
```

We are starting our example with 12,500 labeled images and 37,500 unlabeled images.

Then we initialize the modAL active learner:

```
learner = ActiveLearner(
    estimator=RandomForestClassifier(),
    query_strategy=uncertainty_sampling,
    X_training=X_initial_flat, y_training=y_initial
)
```

In the preceding code snippet, an ActiveLearner object is created. This learner uses RandomForestClassifier as its estimator. RandomForest is a popular ensemble learning method for classification, which operates by constructing multiple decision trees during training and outputting the class that is the mode of the classes of the individual trees. The query strategy is set to **uncertainty sampling**. In uncertainty sampling, the model queries the instances about which it is least certain about classifying and aims at querying the most informative samples, as we saw in *Chapter 2, Designing Query Strategy Frameworks*. Finally, the X_initial_flat initial training data and y_training labels are provided to the learner.

Finally, we simulate the querying of the labels with the following five-iteration loop:

```
for i in range(5):
    query_idx, _ = learner.query(X_unlabeled)
    actual_label = y_all[query_idx[0]]

    print(f"Selected unlabeled query is sample number {query_idx[0]}.
Actual label: {actual_label}")

    learner.teach(X_unlabeled[query_idx].reshape(1, -1), actual_label.
reshape(1,))
    X_unlabeled = np.delete(X_unlabeled, query_idx, axis=0)
    y_all = np.delete(y_all, query_idx)
```

The preceding loop returns the following:

```
Selected unlabeled query is sample number 3100. Actual label: cat
Selected unlabeled query is sample number 7393. Actual label: deer
Selected unlabeled query is sample number 4728. Actual label: horse
Selected unlabeled query is sample number 447. Actual label: deer
Selected unlabeled query is sample number 17968. Actual label: bird
```

The loop represents five iterations of active ML. In each iteration, the model queries the dataset to label new instances. The learner queries the X_unlabeled training data and returns the query_idx index and query_instance instance of the sample it is most uncertain about. Then, the learner is taught using the instance it queried. In a real-world scenario, this step would involve obtaining the label for the queried instance from an oracle (such as a human annotator). However, in this simulated example, the label is directly taken from the y_all dataset.

This example illustrates the process of active ML using modAL, where the model actively queries specific instances to learn from, rather than passively learning from a static dataset.

modAL is a great Python package that allows us to implement complex active ML methods easily. For example, let's create a use case of active ML using the modAL package, specifically focusing on **committee-based** algorithms. In this example, we'll use a committee of classifiers to query the most informative samples from an unlabeled dataset. As a reminder, we defined the *query-by-committee* *approaches* in *Chapter 2, Designing Query Strategy Frameworks*.

For this example, let's use the Iris dataset (*Fisher, R. A.. (1988). Iris. UCI Machine Learning Repository.* `https://doi.org/10.24432/C56C76`), a common choice for classification tasks. The Iris dataset is a classic dataset in machine learning and statistics, often used for demonstrating classification algorithms. The dataset contains 150 samples of iris flowers. Each sample has four features: sepal length, sepal width, petal length, and petal width. These features are measurements in centimeters of the respective parts of the iris plant. There are three species (classes) of iris plants in the dataset: Iris setosa, Iris virginica, and Iris versicolor. Each class has 50 samples, making the dataset evenly balanced among the three classes. The typical task with the Iris dataset is a multiclass classification problem. The goal is to predict the species of an iris plant based on measurements of its sepals and petals.

We will use a committee of K-Nearest Neighbors classifiers. The committee will use the **query-by-committee (QBC) strategy** to select data points about which it has the most disagreement.

We start by loading the Iris dataset (from the datasets available with `scikit-learn`) and creating an initial small labeled dataset and a larger unlabeled dataset:

```
X, y = load_iris(return_X_y=True)
X_labeled, X_unlabeled, y_labeled, y_unlabeled = train_test_split(
    X, y, test_size=0.9, random_state=42)
```

We initialize twenty `ActiveLearner` instances, each with a `RandomForestClassifier`, and combine them into a `Committee`:

```
n_learners = 20
learners = [ActiveLearner(
        estimator=RandomForestClassifier(), X_training=X_labeled, \
        y_training=y_labeled
    ) for _ in range(n_learners)]
committee = Committee(learner_list=learners,
    query_strategy=vote_entropy_sampling)
```

The active ML loop uses the `vote_entropy_sampling` strategy to select the sample about which the committee members disagree the most.

Here is how our active ML loop looks like for five iterations:

```
n_queries = 5
for idx in range(n_queries):
    query_idx, query_instance = committee.query(X_unlabeled)
    print(f"\nSelected unlabeled query is sample number {query_
idx}. We simulate labeling this sample which is labeled as: {y_
unlabeled[query_idx]}")
    committee.teach(X_unlabeled[query_idx], y_unlabeled[query_idx])

    # Remove the queried instance from the pool
    X_unlabeled = np.delete(X_unlabeled, query_idx, axis=0)
```

```
y_unlabeled = np.delete(y_unlabeled, query_idx)
print(f"Number of unlabeled samples is {len(X_unlabeled)}")

# Calculate and print committee score
committee_score = committee.score(X, y)
print(f"Iteration {idx+1}, Committee Score: {committee_score}")
```

The query method of the Committee object is used to select the most informative sample from the unlabeled X_unlabeled dataset. The committee, consisting of multiple learners, uses its internal query strategy, vote_entropy_sampling, to determine which instance in X_unlabeled it finds most valuable for learning.

The selected sample in each iteration is used to teach (retrain) all the committee's learners. After each query, the performance of the committee is evaluated:

```
Selected unlabeled query is sample number [8]. We simulate labeling
this sample which is labeled as: [0]
Number of unlabeled samples is 129
Iteration 1, Committee Score: 0.96

Selected unlabeled query is sample number [125]. We simulate labeling
this sample which is labeled as: [2]
Number of unlabeled samples is 128
Iteration 2, Committee Score: 0.9466666666666667

Selected unlabeled query is sample number [42]. We simulate labeling
this sample which is labeled as: [2]
Number of unlabeled samples is 127
Iteration 3, Committee Score: 0.9466666666666667

Selected unlabeled query is sample number [47]. We simulate labeling
this sample which is labeled as: [1]
Number of unlabeled samples is 126
Iteration 4, Committee Score: 0.9733333333333334

Selected unlabeled query is sample number [95]. We simulate labeling
this sample which is labeled as: [1]
Number of unlabeled samples is 125
Iteration 5, Committee Score: 0.9733333333333334
```

This example demonstrates how to use a committee of learners with modAL to actively improve model performance by querying the most informative samples. The committee's diverse opinions help in selecting samples that are more informative for learning, thus improving the overall model more efficiently. We observe in our output, for example, that the committee score improved from 0.96 to 0.973.

In active ML, especially when using a committee-based approach as in the preceding example, the expectation is generally that the performance of the model (or in this case, the committee of models) will improve over the iterations. This improvement is expected because the committee is being trained on increasingly informative samples, which are selected based on the committee's uncertainty or disagreement.

However, a few points are worth noting:

- **Incremental improvement**: The increase in performance might not be linear or consistent across all iterations. In some iterations, the model may improve significantly, while in others, the improvement might be minimal or even stagnant. We can see this in our example, where the committee score went from 0.96 to 0.94, and then back up to 0.973.

- **Depends on data and model**: The rate and consistency of improvement depend on the nature of the data and the effectiveness of the learning algorithm. For some datasets or configurations, the improvement might be rapid and consistent, while for others, it might be slower or less predictable.

- **Diminishing returns**: As the most informative samples are added to the training set, the remaining unlabeled samples may become less informative, leading to diminishing returns in terms of performance improvement in later iterations.

- **Performance metric**: The committee score (be it accuracy or another metric; in our case, the modAL function uses the accuracy by default) is a measure of how well the committee's combined prediction aligns with the true labels. As the committee is exposed to more representative samples of the data, its predictions should become more accurate.

- **Evaluation method**: The method of evaluating the committee's performance can also affect perceived improvements. If the evaluation is done on a static test set, the improvements may be more evident. However, if the evaluation is on the training set (including newly added samples), the improvements might be less pronounced due to increasing complexity or variance in the data.

In summary, while an increase in the committee's performance score over a number of iterations is a common expectation in active ML, the actual pattern of improvement can vary based on various factors. Regular monitoring and adjustments might be necessary to ensure the active ML process is yielding the desired results, as we saw in *Chapter 6*, *Evaluating and Enhancing Efficiency*.

The choice of the right Python package for active ML depends on the specific requirements of the task at hand, including the type of data, the ML model being used, and the desired active learning strategy. Integrating these packages effectively can lead to more efficient data labeling, faster model convergence, and overall better performance of ML models.

Next, we will explore tools that can be easily used to perform active ML on unlabeled data such as Encord Active, Lightly, Cleanlab, Voxel51, and UBIAI.

Getting familiar with the active ML tools

Throughout this book, we've introduced and discussed several key active ML tools and labeling platforms, including Lightly, Encord, LabelBox, Snorkel AI, Prodigy, modAL, and Roboflow. To further enhance your understanding and assist you in selecting the most suitable tool for your specific project needs, let's revisit these tools with expanded insights and introduce a few additional ones:

- **modAL** (`https://modal-python.readthedocs.io/en/latest/`): This is a flexible and modular active ML framework in Python, designed to seamlessly integrate with `scikit-learn`. It stands out for its extensive range of query strategies, which can be tailored to various active ML scenarios. Whether you are dealing with classification, regression, or clustering tasks, modAL provides a robust and intuitive interface for implementing active learning workflows.

- **Label Studio** (`https://docs.humansignal.com/guide/active_learning.html?__hstc=90244869.a32555b92661e36e5f4b3b8a0f2cc99a.170621 0819596.1706210819596.1706210819596.1&__hssc=90244869.2.1706 210819596&__hsfp=3755259113&_gl=1*1i1r2ib*_ga*MTE1NzM0NDQ4Ny 4xNzA2MjEwODE5*_ga_NQELN45JRH*MTcwNjIxMDgxOS4xLjEuMTcwNj IxMDgzNC4wLjAuMA`): An open source, multi-type data labeling tool, Label Studio excels in its adaptability to different forms of data, including text, images, and audio. It allows for the integration of ML models into the labeling process, thereby enhancing labeling efficiency through active ML. Its flexibility extends to customizable labeling interfaces, making it suitable for a broad range of applications in data annotation.

- **Prodigy** (`https://prodi.gy/`): Prodigy offers a unique blend of active ML and human-in-the-loop approaches. It's a highly efficient annotation tool, particularly for refining training data for NLP models. Its real-time feedback loop allows for rapid iteration and model improvement, making it an ideal choice for projects that require quick adaptation and precision in data annotation.

- **Lightly**(`https://www.lightly.ai/`): Specializing in image datasets, Lightly uses active ML to identify the most representative and diverse set of images for training. This ensures that models are trained on a balanced and varied dataset, leading to improved generalization and performance. Lightly is particularly useful for projects where data is abundant but labeling resources are limited.

- **Encord Active** (`https://encord.com/active`): Focused on active ML for image and video data, Encord Active is integrated within a comprehensive labeling platform. It streamlines the labeling process by identifying and prioritizing the most informative samples, thereby enhancing efficiency and reducing the manual annotation workload. This platform is particularly beneficial for large-scale computer vision projects.

- **Cleanlab** (`https://cleanlab.ai/`): Cleanlab stands out for its ability to detect, quantify, and rectify label errors in datasets. This capability is invaluable for active ML, where the quality of the labeled data directly impacts model performance. It offers a systematic approach to ensuring data integrity, which is crucial for training robust and reliable models.

- **Voxel51** (`https://voxel51.com/blog/supercharge-your-annotation-workflow-with-active-learning`): With a focus on video and image data, Voxel51 provides an active ML platform that prioritizes the most informative data for labeling. This enhances the annotation workflow, making it more efficient and effective. The platform is particularly adept at handling complex, large-scale video datasets, offering powerful tools for video analytics and ML

- **UBIAI** (`https://ubiai.tools/active-learning-2`): UBIAI is a tool that specializes in text annotation and supports active ML. It simplifies the process of training and deploying NLP models by streamlining the annotation workflow. Its active ML capabilities ensure that the most informative text samples are prioritized for annotation, thus improving model accuracy with fewer labeled examples.

- **Snorkel AI** (`https://snorkel.ai`): Renowned for its novel approach to creating, modeling, and managing training data, Snorkel AI uses a technique called weak supervision. This method combines various labeling sources to reduce the dependency on large labeled datasets, complementing active ML strategies to create efficient training data pipelines.

- **Deepchecks** (`https://deepchecks.com/importance-of-active-learning-in-machine-learning`): Deepchecks offers a comprehensive suite of validation checks that are essential in an active ML context. These checks ensure the quality and diversity of datasets and models, thereby facilitating the development of more accurate and robust ML systems. It's an essential tool for maintaining data integrity and model reliability throughout the ML lifecycle.

- **LabelBox** (`https://labelbox.com/guides/the-guide-to-getting-started-with-active-learning`): As a comprehensive data labeling platform, LabelBox excels in managing the entire data labeling process. It provides a suite of tools for creating, managing, and iterating on labeled data, applicable to a wide range of data types such as images, videos, and text. Its support for active learning methodologies further enhances the efficiency of the labeling process, making it an ideal choice for large-scale ML projects.

- **Roboflow** (`https://docs.roboflow.com/api-reference/active-learning`): Designed for computer vision projects, Roboflow streamlines the process of preparing image data. It is especially valuable for tasks involving image recognition and object detection. Roboflow's focus on easing the preparation, annotation, and management of image data makes it a key resource for teams and individuals working in the field of computer vision.

Each tool in this extended list brings unique capabilities to the table, addressing specific challenges in ML projects. From image and video annotation to text processing and data integrity checks, these tools provide the necessary functionalities to enhance project efficiency and efficacy through active ML strategies.

Summary

This chapter has provided a comprehensive exploration of the various Python libraries, frameworks, and tools essential for active ML. By navigating through the intricacies of popular libraries such as `scikit-learn` and `modAL`, we have explored their capabilities and how they can be effectively applied in active ML scenarios. Additionally, this chapter has expanded your toolkit by introducing a range of other active ML tools, each with its own unique features and potential applications.

Whether you are a beginner taking your first steps in active ML or an experienced programmer seeking to refine your skills, this chapter aimed to equip you with a solid foundation in the tools and techniques of active ML. The knowledge gained here is not just theoretical; it is a practical guide to help you master Python packages for enhanced active ML and to familiarize yourself with a broad spectrum of active ML tools. This understanding will enable you to select and apply the most appropriate tools for your specific ML projects, enhancing the efficiency and effectiveness of your models.

Congratulations! You have reached the end of the book. But remember you have just started your journey in the world of active ML. As you move forward in your ML journey, remember that the field of active ML is continually evolving. Staying informed about new developments, tools, and techniques will be key to maintaining a cutting-edge approach in your work. The tools and concepts covered in this chapter provide a strong basis for further exploration and innovation in the exciting and dynamic field of active ML.

Index

A

active learning
versus passive learning 13, 14
active machine learning
(active ML) **3, 115-117, 131, 132**
components 5
definition 4
implementing, for image
classification project 66
loop 6
methods 131
used, for enhancing production
model monitoring 128
using, for segmentation project 84-88
active ML, applications 4
anomaly detection 5
computer vision applications 4
medical diagnosis 5
natural language tasks 4
recommendation systems 5
active ML, for image classification project
CNN, building for CIFAR dataset 67-73
uncertainty sampling, applying to improve
classification performance 73- 76
active ML pipelines
monitoring 124-127

active ML run
cessation, determining 127, 128
active ML, to object detection project
applying 76
evaluation metrics, analyzing 79, 80
model, preparing and training 77-79
strategy, implementing 80-83
active ML, tools
Cleanlab 146
Deepchecks 146
Encord Active 145
LabelBox 146
Label Studio 145
Lightly 145
modAL 145
Prodigy 145
Roboflow 146
Snorkel AI 146
UBIAI 146
Voxel51 146
Adam 71
annotation quality
annotator skills, assessing 57
balanced sampling 59-61
multiple annotators, using 58, 59
average KL divergence 30-34

AWS EC2 on-demand pricing
reference link 122

C

CIFAR dataset
CNN, building for 67-73
Cleanlab
reference link 146
ClearML
reference link 125
cloud-hosted active ML pipeline
creating 122-124
example 122
committee-based algorithms 141
comprehensive logging 124
convolutional neural network (CNN)
building, for CIFAR dataset 67-73

D

data drift 129
data drift detection 132, 133
Dataloop
reference link 51
decision boundary 18
Deepchecks
reference link 146
density-weighted sampling methods 38-43
advantages 42, 43
techniques 40, 41

E

EMC sampling
advantages 36
labeling with 34-36

Encord
reference link 51
Encord Active
reference link 145
entropy sampling 23
expected error reduction (EER) 17
sampling with 37, 38
technique, advantages 38
expected gradient length (EGL) 35
expected model change (EMC) 17

F

frames per second (FPS) 91
frames, with Lightly
selecting, to label for object detection 93
frame with Lightly, selecting to label for object detection
active ML run, scheduling 97-100
dataset and pre-trained model 93, 94
inference 95-97
required Lightly files, creating 94, 95
worker and active ML run 101-114

H

human-in-the-loop labeling tools
exploring 50, 51
labeling platforms 51
human-in-the-loop systems
managing 55, 56

I

image classification project
active ML, implementing for 66
image sequences 50

informative frames
selecting, with Lightly 92
instance segmentation 84
interactive learning systems and workflows
designing 46-50
intersection over union (IoU) 79

K

Kullback-Leibler divergence
(KL divergence) 30

L

LabelBox
reference link 51, 146
labeling interface 46
labeling ontology 49
Label Studio
reference link 145
least-confidence sampling 19
Lightly
reference link 145
URL 91
used, for selecting most
informative frames 92
using, for self-supervised
learning (SSL) 115-117
loss function 71

M

machine learning (ML) 5, 89
margin sampling 20
Mask R-CNN 84
maximum disagreement 26-28

membership query synthesis 7
advantages 8
disadvantages 8
ML models
implementing, for video analysis 90, 91
MobileNet
reference link 68
modAL 136, 139
for enhanced active ML 139-144
reference link 139, 145
model decay 129
detection 132, 133
model-label disagreements
handling 52
manual review of conflicts 54
mismatches, identifying
programmatically 52-54
model output change (MOC) 35
MongoDB
reference link 126

N

natural language processing (NLP) 90
reference link 51
neural networks (NNs) 24

O

optimizer 71
oracle 4, 5

P

Panoptic FPN 84
passive learning
versus active learning 13, 14

pool-based sampling 11
  advantages 12
  challenges 12
principal component analysis (PCA) 92
proactive monitoring 124
Prodigy
  reference link 51, 145
production model monitoring
  active ML 130-132
  challenges 128-130
  data drift detection 132, 133
  enhancing, with active ML 128
  model decay detection 132, 133
PyTorch data loader 69

Q

query-by-committee
  approaches 25, 26
query-by-committee, approaches
  average KL divergence 30-34
  maximum disagreement 26-28
  vote entropy 28-30
query-by-committee (QBC) strategy 142
query strategies 17
query strategies, scenarios
  exploring 7
  membership query synthesis 7, 8
  pool-based sampling 11, 12
  stream-based selective sampling 8-10

R

ratio of confidence method 21
ResNet
  reference link 68
RMSprop 71
Roboflow
  reference link 146

S

scikit-learn 136
  for enhanced active ML 136-139
  reference link 136
segmentation project
  active ML, using for 84-88
self-supervised learning (SSL)
  Lightly, using for 115-117
Snorkel AI
  reference link 51, 146
stochastic gradient descent (SGD) 71
stream-based selective sampling 8-10
  advantages 10
  drawbacks 10
support vector machines (SVMs) 24
systematic biases 54

T

T-distributed stochastic neighbor
    embedding (TSNE) 92
traditional machine learning
  reasons, for expensive labeling 13

U

UBIAI
reference link 146
uncertainty sampling methods 59, 140
exploring 18-24
**uniform manifold approximation
and projection (UMAP) 92**
unlabeled dataset 5
unnormalizing 71

V

video analysis
ML models, implementing for 90, 91
vote entropy 28-30
Voxel51
reference link 146

W

workflow 47

Y

YOLACT 84

packtpub.com

Subscribe to our online digital library for full access to over 7,000 books and videos, as well as industry leading tools to help you plan your personal development and advance your career. For more information, please visit our website.

Why subscribe?

- Spend less time learning and more time coding with practical eBooks and Videos from over 4,000 industry professionals

- Improve your learning with Skill Plans built especially for you

- Get a free eBook or video every month

- Fully searchable for easy access to vital information

- Copy and paste, print, and bookmark content

Did you know that Packt offers eBook versions of every book published, with PDF and ePub files available? You can upgrade to the eBook version at packtpub.com and as a print book customer, you are entitled to a discount on the eBook copy. Get in touch with us at customercare@packtpub.com for more details.

At www.packtpub.com, you can also read a collection of free technical articles, sign up for a range of free newsletters, and receive exclusive discounts and offers on Packt books and eBooks.

Other Books You May Enjoy

If you enjoyed this book, you may be interested in these other books by Packt:

Practical Machine Learning on Databricks

Debu Sinha

ISBN: 978-1-80181-203-0

- Transition smoothly from DIY setups to databricks
- Master AutoML for quick ML experiment setup
- Automate model retraining and deployment
- Leverage databricks feature store for data prep
- Use MLflow for effective experiment tracking
- Gain practical insights for scalable ML solutions
- Find out how to handle model drifts in production environments

Machine Learning Security with Azure

Georgia Kalyva

ISBN: 978-1-80512-048-3

- Explore the Azure Machine Learning project life cycle and services
- Assess the vulnerability of your ML assets using the Zero Trust model
- Explore essential controls to ensure data governance and compliance in Azure
- Understand different methods to secure your data, models, and infrastructure against attacks
- Find out how to detect and remediate past or ongoing attacks
- Explore methods to recover from a security breach
- Monitor and maintain your security posture with the right tools and best practices

Packt is searching for authors like you

If you're interested in becoming an author for Packt, please visit `authors.packtpub.com` and apply today. We have worked with thousands of developers and tech professionals, just like you, to help them share their insight with the global tech community. You can make a general application, apply for a specific hot topic that we are recruiting an author for, or submit your own idea.

Share Your Thoughts

Now you've finished *Active Machine Learning with Python*, we'd love to hear your thoughts! Scan the QR code below to go straight to the Amazon review page for this book and share your feedback or leave a review on the site that you purchased it from.

`https://packt.link/r/1835464947`

Your review is important to us and the tech community and will help us make sure we're delivering excellent quality content.

Download a free PDF copy of this book

Thanks for purchasing this book!

Do you like to read on the go but are unable to carry your print books everywhere?

Is your eBook purchase not compatible with the device of your choice?

Don't worry, now with every Packt book you get a DRM-free PDF version of that book at no cost.

Read anywhere, any place, on any device. Search, copy, and paste code from your favorite technical books directly into your application.

The perks don't stop there, you can get exclusive access to discounts, newsletters, and great free content in your inbox daily

Follow these simple steps to get the benefits:

1. Scan the QR code or visit the link below

https://packt.link/free-ebook/9781835464946

2. Submit your proof of purchase
3. That's it! We'll send your free PDF and other benefits to your email directly

www.ingramcontent.com/pod-product-compliance
Lightning Source LLC
Chambersburg PA
CBHW080531060326
40690CB00022B/5096